GAMES FOR GROWTH

EDUCATIONAL GAMES IN THE CLASSROOM

ALICE KAPLAN GORDON

Science Research Associates, Inc., College Division
165 University Avenue, Palo Alto, California 94301

A Subsidiary of IBM

The term "game" connotes fun.

And activities that are fun seem to be incompatible

with activities that are serious.

Everyone knows that education is

a serious business . . .

The fundamental deficiency of the school system

is its failure to motivate the youth of the country to want to learn.

This is probably due as much to the methodology used

as it is to the fact that what the schools teach is perceived to have

little connection with the real world . . .

Of the many educational innovations,

games and simulations offer great promise

of transforming the classroom

from an assembly of passive, if not bored spectators

into a laboratory of active participants

in the learning process . . .

A game is essentially

a simplified slice of reality.

Its structure reflects a real-world process

that the designer wishes to teach or investigate;

the game serves as a vehicle for testing

that process or for learning

more about its working . . .

In playing games, students tend to develop feelings

of effectiveness and control,

because the actions

they take in the game produce results . . .

There is no way to remake

or cultivate attitudes

in one grandiose stroke;

but teachers can help students

to study them by

providing opportunities for

actually playing out their

implications and effects in

classroom situations . . .

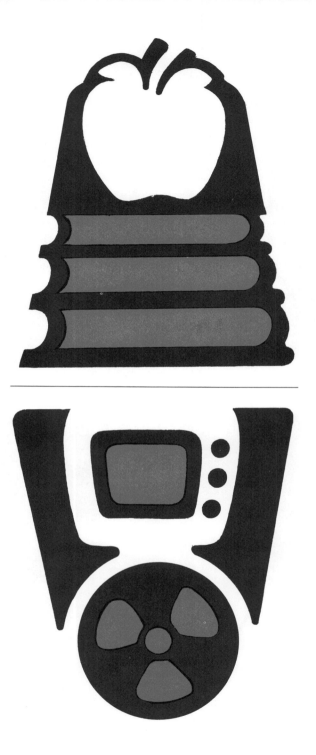

Nobody suggests that

games should be used all the time

to teach all things.

But if they are as effective in

altering attitudes and teaching processes

as has been suggested,

all other media

can be utilized more

effectively . . .

Contents

Credits

The Sierra Leone Game, page 57, The Sumerian Game, page 102, and The Free Enterprise Game, page 103, were produced by the U.S. Office of Education, Bureau of Research, Project 2841.

The development of Machinist, page 100, was supported by a subcontract between Harvard University and Abt Associates. This subcontract was financed by Grant #OEG-1-6-061819-2240, a contract between Harvard University and the U.S. Office of Education.

CHAPTER 1

EDUCATION IS CHILD'S PLAY

1

Origin and History of Games

The Game Approach

Current Uses of Games

Nobody is satisfied with education these days, and surely that discontent is a good thing. It is not that our schools are so bad, necessarily, but that we earnestly wish to make them better. Individualized instruction and team teaching, language labs and computers, new math and sociology, ungraded classes and ungraded subjects — in short, new methods, new materials, new subjects, and new goals — are being tried all over the United States.

The burgeoning of curriculum projects, an index of these efforts, reflects two basic trends. First, relevance to current issues has been a key criterion in the selection of materials designed to revitalize the curriculum. Second, the development of new methods of presenting the materials, appropriate to the substantive content, has become a consistent aim of curriculum developers. This approach follows the philosophy, expounded by Bruner, that the student ought to participate in the methodology of a discipline and not merely absorb its content. On the basis of their experience and intuition, educators can testify to the effectiveness of learning experiences where the student takes an active part.

Efforts to upgrade the system have made their mark. If recent innovations have not yet altered the fundamental structure of the school system, they have changed its image. The quiet, well-disciplined class, obediently learning in time-honored ways what somebody once decided was important, no longer represents the norm. Quite the opposite. The classroom is being converted from an assembly of passive, perhaps bored, spectators into a laboratory where each member is an active participant in the learning process.

Among recent innovations, educational games offer great promise of furthering this change. Not only are they fun, but they require that all players share in making decisions throughout the game. Unfortunately, educational games are not well understood. They are not yet widely available, and experience with them is necessarily limited; as a result, a mystique surrounds the technique. To complicate matters, the use of games implies a seeming irreverence toward education.

Educational games are neither esoteric nor frivolous. But they differ enough from most other classroom activities to raise questions about the role of the teacher, the time and space required, how to evaluate what games teach students, and the benefits and drawbacks of using games. These and other operational problems will be discussed in ensuing chapters. But the primary question remains: Can educational games, which often resemble entertainment games, be employed for serious purposes in the classroom? A survey of the origin and history of serious games may help allay initial doubts about the viability of the technique.

Origin and History of Serious Games

The term *game* connotes fun. And activities that are fun seem to be incompatible with activities that are serious. To reconcile the two ideas, one need only recall observing two devoted chess players engrossed in developing strategies to win the game. In athletic competitions, too, players are often fiercely dedicated to winning; at times their very livelihood depends on victory. But *serious* is not used here to refer to the attitude players assume when they participate in a game. Rather, it refers to the purpose of a game. Chess, no matter how seriously it is taken, exists for the entertainment of its devotees. Serious games, no matter how much fun they are, have as their primary purpose something other than the entertainment of the players.

The use of games for education, training, research, and planning derives from some basic observations about entertainment games. In general, the latter are based on real-world activities. Chess, for example, was consciously developed as a representation of war more than 2000 years ago. The game of Monopoly,® created during the depression of the 1930's, reflected popular thinking about how the economy worked. The opportunity for players to buy and sell property in a make-believe fashion, at a time when many of them were unable to do so in the real world, contributed to the game's great success. Political games, such as Diplomacy, allow players to make top-level decisions in the international arena.

The fun of these games lies in the combination of reality and make-believe. Players enjoy exercising power, negotiating, making decisions — especially in spheres of activity where their real-world influence is negligible. And it is all safe. The worst that can happen is that one goes bankrupt in a make-believe world, or one's make-believe country is defeated. In short, the penalty for errors of judgment is losing the game.

War Games

No such luxury is available to men who make crucial decisions in the real world. The wrong move in a war, for example, can have catastrophic results. Yet, no simple formulas dictate infallible courses of action in given situations. No two situations are precisely the same, and each requires decisions tailored to its unique circumstances. The idea of practicing war is obviously absurd. The best one can hope to do is learn from other people's experience and one's own. But the best is not good enough.

It was the "harmless" aspect of games that led to their use for serious purposes in that most harmful of activities, war. The Germans were the first to exploit games for research and training. In the nineteenth century, members of the German General Staff recognized that games could be used to represent and work out real military situations, thereby avoiding the problems of logistics, time, and money involved in actually moving armies around in the field. As a first step, the military conflict represented in the game had to be analyzed. The actors in the game had to be defined and their relative strengths indicated in the form of material resources. Constraints on their actions in the real world—such as how fast armies could move over the terrain, how effective different weapons were, what forces were required to hold territory—were defined in the rules of the game. Chance elements, such as weather conditions and surprise attacks, could also be introduced. Markers symbolizing the forces belonging to different nations were moved about on a map. Later, sand tables were introduced as a means of showing terrain. By experimenting with strategies in different situations, the effectiveness of alternative war plans could be tested at almost no cost. The games gave officers additional training in analyzing military situations, and helped sharpen their decision-making abilities. An effective laboratory for war had been developed.

During World War II, the game approach was used to find quick and effective solutions to urgent and complex problems. The technique of experimenting with different plans of action, derived from war gaming, was applied to the military problems at hand. It was known, for example, that German submarines traveled in packs of twelve. The total number of torpedoes that the whole pack could fire was fixed. The maximum number of ships that the Allies could expect to lose in any convoy was therefore also fixed. If a smaller number of larger convoys was deployed, any convoy would still confront only the same twelve German submarines. Consequently, while actual losses might remain the same, the effect of those losses would be reduced. The loss of ten ships out of fifty was more serious than ten ships out of two hundred. Fortunately for the Allies, the Germans did not alter the size of their submarine packs.

This type of analysis, known as Operations Research, was also applied to less critical problems. An Operations Research worker on a new assignment noticed that much time was wasted while soldiers waited to wash and rinse their mess kits after eating. Four tubs were used — two for washing, two for rinsing. After observing that, on the average, washing the kit took three times as long as rinsing it, the O.R. worker suggested that three tubs be used for washing and one for rinsing. With that change, waiting lines were eliminated.

What do these examples have to do with games? One can visualize either solution being arrived at in a game situation. In the first, two players, representing German and Allied forces, would be sufficient. The objective of the German player would be to destroy as many Allied ships as possible. The rules might state that his submarines could travel only in packs of twelve, and he would be told how many torpedoes the subs might fire, at what range, and with what destructive force. The Allied player would be given targets, and permitted to deploy ships in any numbers to win his targets. When encounters between ships and subs occurred, losses could be determined according to a given schedule — as in poker, where a straight flush beats four of a kind, which beats a full house, and so on. If two ships met twelve subs, for example, the ships would automatically be destroyed. The Allied player would have the problem of deploying enough ships to win a given target even if the submarine pack knocked out the maximum number it was capable of destroying. Since the Allied player would probably be given fewer ships than he needed to win all his targets, he would have to allocate his ships carefully, using only the minimum number possible for any given target. After experimenting, he might find the optimum convoy size to satisfy all conditions in the game; that is, the smallest number of ships sufficient to win the targets, even if reduced by maximum submarine destructive capability.

The second situation could also be gamed. One player competing against a given standard would be sufficient. His objective might be to maximize the number of hours his soldiers spent in the field by minimizing the number of hours required for other tasks. Time would have to be allowed for cooking meals, for each soldier to eat three meals and clean up afterwards, for cleaning barracks, and for other routines. The rules might also state that each soldier had to make his own bed, wash and rinse his own mess kit, and so forth to prevent divisions of labor that would complicate the game too much. By experimenting with different arrangements, the player could find the optimum solution for keeping the greatest number of men in the field for the longest possible time. Scoring the game could resemble scoring in an amusement-park rifle game, where one is rated "marksman," "sharpshooter," "expert," depending on the number of points one gets. In this game, the number of hours soldiers spend in the field would be translated into ratings ranging from "well-trained" through "poorly trained."

The descriptions above could be developed into entertaining games for the general public. For the men who had to solve the military problems, though, the task provided little enough amusement. For them, games represented a method of analyzing problems, and an opportunity to experiment with solutions and evaluate their effectiveness without the potentially dangerous consequences of a mistake in the real world.

Business Games

After World War II, the game technique was applied to another area of human endeavor where the stakes are high — business. Mistakes in business can be ruinous. Often the consequences of an investment decision are not apparent for years. By then, much profit and productivity — and the opportunity to correct the mistake — may have been lost. Meanwhile, one uncorrected bad judgment has probably led to others.

How does a businessman learn to make wise decisions? Pat answers will not work because conditions of uncertainty operate in the business world as they do in the military. Competitors' strategies change. Prices rise and fall. The labor supply varies. Credit may be tight or easy. Technological changes are introduced. Market demand varies. A good decision today might be a disastrous one tomorrow.

Games provide an opportunity for businessmen to experiment with different decisions under different conditions. Whether a player takes the most conservative or the most radical course of action in a game situation, the results are innocuous. Nothing has been lost. On the contrary, much has been gained for the businessman can evaluate the consequences of his decision in a few hours instead of several costly years. Perhaps the game allows him to investigate the consequences of a proposed merger with another corporation. Perhaps he wishes to experiment with strategies to beat his competitors. The rules of management games can be tailored to a variety of business situations.

In one business game, players portray either public relations executives for competing banks or salesmen for different advertising media. The bankers' objective is to allocate their advertising budgets so that the greatest number of people is reached with the greatest impact. The salesmen's objective is to sell the most advertising. All the players have information about the economic and social profile of their hypothetical city. The various banks have different types of clients, some being predominantly workingmen's banks, others being more aristocratic. All are planning campaigns advertising automobile loans to the public. All bankers and all salesmen negotiate with each other in turn. At the end of a playing cycle, each banker fills out his order, perhaps dividing it among primetime television and billboard ads, radio time or newspaper ads, and home circulars. The winner among the salesmen is the one who sells the most advertising. The winning banker is the one who invests in the most effective combination of advertising media, as determined by a schedule of number of people reached and the presumed influence on them. The game does not purport to teach bankers the best advertising strategy for all time. Nobody knows that. But it does give them practice in weighing the factors that are important in making an intelligent decision.

Consider business situations in which human interactions are particularly important. Can one learn to sell or administer from books and lectures? Most salesmen and administrators would agree that experience is their best teacher, but it is an expensive one. Games reduce the cost of experience by providing opportunities to practice, to learn by doing, to make mistakes and profit by them all with very little expenditure of time and money.

A game to train salesmen, for example, could be constructed quite easily. Thirty players could be divided into two groups: salesmen and prospective clients. The salesmen's first task would be to plan a day's appointments, with the object of seeing the largest number of likely prospects for the lowest traveling costs. The appointments made, salesmen would visit their contacts and give their pitch. Perhaps a salesman would get so involved with one client that, late for his next appointment, he finds that another salesman has arrived before him. At the end of a "day," prospective clients could be asked to decide what they are going to buy and from whom. The salesman whose total sales are the highest is, of course, the winner. Why clients chose him would be important; the buyer's evaluation of the salesmen's performance would be the crucial learning derived from the game. After one playing, the roles might be reversed. The sales trainees would thus have the chance both to practice their art and to evaluate each other from the buyer's side of the desk.

Another possibility is a game dealing with personnel relations in industry, though the following description can be applied in other areas. The actors in the game might be a Personnel Manager, the Department Manager, the Vice-President who has ultimate responsibility for the department, and several employees. Among them are John and Jim. John is unpopular, efficient, and irreplaceable. Jim is popular but inefficient; he works with John. John and Jim have been getting on increasingly badly, and the employees in the department are taking sides. As a result of the staff's involvement in the problem, the department's efficiency is being decreased. The Department Manager is not included in office politics since staff members are reluctant to complain upwards. The Personnel Manager and Vice-President are aware that something is wrong, since productivity is falling and complaints have been received from clients. John, the efficient, wishes to get rid of Jim, the inefficient. Jim would like to do the work he is doing but not with John. Unfortunately, no other openings in his kind of work are available. The Department Manager visits the employees at intervals and, in turn, is visited by the Vice-President and the Personnel Manager. The latter two may go directly to the employees if they feel that the Department Manager is not solving the problems, but they risk offending him. The Department Manager gains maximum points for resolving the situation without recourse to the Personnel Manager or Vice-President. However, if he does not seek their aid and does not succeed in resolving the dispute, he loses heavily. Obviously, there is no single right answer in this game situation. Its main value is in providing the opportunity to struggle with the problem, and to rapidly evaluate a solution from the viewpoints of all parties involved.

Games, then, represent an approach or method of solving serious problems. A definition and examination of a technique used for such sophisticated purposes would illuminate the reasons for its success.

The Game Approach

What Games Are

The best way to define a game would be to play one first, and analyze it later. Under the circumstances, a written description will have to suffice. A game may be defined as any simulated contest (play) among adversaries (players) operating under constraints (rules) for an objective (winning).

Serious games are characterized by two basic features. First, they usually simulate real-life situations which many formal games, such as card games, do not. This distinction is not hard and fast, however, since games similar to card games could be used to teach mathematics. Second, serious games are seldom pure competitions where one person wins and everyone else loses. The cooperative aspect of most real-life situations is built into games and winning is usually a relative thing. Several people or teams may be more successful than the other players. This is not merely a euphemistic way of avoiding the idea of losing. In the personnel-relations game, for example, who could be considered the winner? If the conflict is resolved effectively, in essence everybody wins. In the salesmen's game, the man who sells the most wins, but that doesn't mean everybody else loses. The winner has simply had the greatest success relative to the others.

The evaluation of success is not, however, the most crucial outcome of a game. The aspect of winning does serve to motivate players by appealing to the competitive urge. And it does present a clearly defined objective that players work toward. But the means that players employ in attempting to win are far more important than the specific goal achieved.

The basic theory behind serious games explains why this is so. A game is essentially a simplified slice of reality. Its structure reflects a real-world process that the designer wishes to teach or investigate; the game serves as a vehicle for testing that process or for learning more about its workings. For example, a game designed to teach students the basic principles of supply and demand would represent a simple model of how the economy works. In one such game, called Market, players assume the roles of wholesalers, retailers, and consumers. The consumers must all buy certain essential goods, and may also choose freely among other items. The object of the wholesalers and retailers is to sell as much as they can at the highest profit. At first, wholesalers and retailers may set prices on their goods in a random fashion. During play, however, it becomes apparent that whether or not their prices are too high depends partly on how many people want to buy their goods and how badly. By the time the game is over, students understand the basic mechanism of supply and demand, although they may not know the label for it.

Because the economic process is built into the game structure, students—by making concrete decisions about what to do as they play—learn how the process works. This method of learning seems superior to abstract descriptions of economic principles, which are far removed from the students' experience.

Underlying all games is a model of the process they are meant to simulate. A model is a representation of objects or events that correspond to real objects or events. The model defines and structures the relations between the various objects; for example, a chemical equation is a model describing the interaction of two or more chemicals. The game of Market is based on an economic model that describes the relation between the supply of goods and the demand for them, as it affects prices.

In developing a game for research purposes, one first builds a model of the process to be studied, as far as it could be defined. To study how labor unions acquired support from an initially neutral population, the researcher would first build a model that defined the actors in the process and the relations between them. The basic actors are management personnel, labor organizers, and uncommitted laborers. The objective of management is to prevent unionization by retaining the loyalty of the laboring population. The objective of the labor organizers is to get the greatest number of employees to join the union. The objective of the laborers is to get the best deal for themselves through any channels. Management has various possible ways of keeping labor loyal, such as raising wages and improving working conditions. For the organizers, promises and perhaps coercion are possible ways of acquiring support. Labor merely needs to remain passive and be persuaded by either side.

The researcher would have this game played many times, and would do a statistical analysis of the outcomes. The techniques that were most effective with various kinds of populations could be determined, and a detailed model could then be built for use in further research. The same game could, of course, be used to teach students about the unionization process.

To sum up, a game is a simplified representation of a dynamic real-world process. This process usually involves competition and cooperation, which are also the pivotal elements in the game situation.

Game Formats

Educational games fall into two basic patterns: board games and role-play games. The format selected depends on the subject of a game, and the purpose or population for which it is designed.

Board Games. Many classroom games resemble commercial entertainment games in that they are built around a gameboard on which most of the action takes place. In Monopoly, the materials required for play are a board, play money, deeds, and tokens representing houses and hotels. In educational games, the same type of presentation is used when the game is intended to graphically represent the process under study.

In the elementary school game of Neighborhood, for example, students develop a geographical area, shown as a grid, by putting down tokens representing people, factories, stores, cultural centers. Each cycle of play represents twenty years; population is considered to increase geometrically so that, after several cycles, the board fills up with people and the facilities required for their sustenance and entertainment. Eventually, when geographical obstacles such as swamps have been cleared and no land space remains, players must begin to build up to accommodate the population and to expand facilities. By the end of the game, students have seen the course of development graphically represented on the board.

Role-play Games. The second basic structure, role playing, is used primarily in games that teach processes involving much negotiation, bargaining, compromise; in general, human interaction. The labor-management or unionization game, as outlined above, would probably best lend itself to a role-play format. This type of game usually requires only written materials in the form of a scenario and profiles. The scenario is used to set the scene, to describe the background for the action. In the unionization game, information about the company, working conditions, the personalities involved, and general economic conditions, if relevant, would all be included. The scenario is likely to be fictional, and perhaps amusing, to help players imagine themselves operating in the situation described.

All players receive the same scenario, but each receives a unique profile describing his specific personality; his relationship to other players ("You went to public school with your boss and remember him as teacher's pet. You hated him then and hate him now though your fellow employees don't feel that way about him"); his specific objectives in the game ("The thing you want most is to undermine your boss's position even if it means sacrificing some benefit for yourself" or "What you want is to improve your position so you can afford to send your kids to college. You don't care how you do it, union or not, so long as you do it"); and how he feels about conditions described in the scenario. These profiles are probably one or two pages long, and are meant to give the player some basis for responding to situations as they arise in the game. In the course of play, though usually not foreseen at the outset, conflicts between various players are revealed and natural alliances evolve. In the unionization game, negotiations between management and labor, and between organizers and labor, would precede each cycle. At the end of each cycle, new information (in the form of announcements, perhaps) about economic conditions in the industry could be introduced to complicate the

decisions each team has to make. For example, the labor organizers, who are also employees, would probably have the
added problem of keeping their identity secret to avoid repri-
sals on the part of management.

Rules are the only other materials required. These rules
would set forth, in broad terms, the objectives of all categories
of players ("Management: prevent unionization at the least
cost to you"). The rules would also define what kinds of actions are allowed or disallowed ("Management: You may fire
anybody you suspect of being an organizer but you'd better
be sure. If you're wrong, you're likely to arouse the wrath of
your other employees").

Hybrids. Many games are combinations of the board and role-
playing techniques. In Monopoly,® the basic action of the game
is played out on the board, but some negotiations may occur
in buying property from other players. In role-play games, a
board can be used to record the action. In a city-planning
game, for example, players might have to negotiate to rede-
velop a destroyed area of the city, constrained by what exists
in the untouched areas. An alternative plan might be tried in
each cycle; an industrial area could develop in a formerly
residential one, or a middle-class residential area might replace a slum. Players could use the gameboard to observe an
overall plan until consensus is reached at the end of the game.

Games and Simulations

A term frequently heard in the trade is *simulation.* On occa-
sion, the word has been used because it sounds more serious
than *game.* Perhaps it is felt that educators are more likely to
be interested in the technique if all traces of frivolity are eliminated. *Simulation* is simply the more encompassing term. All
games are simulations; not all simulations are games.

The basic difference is this: In a game, a winner is usually
identified; a simulation need not have a winner. The distinction
is minor, not universally agreed upon, and probably interesting
only to professional designers. However, one implication of
the distinction is worth examining.

Consider a simulation of Congress, focusing on one issue:
whether or not to raise taxes. Students would be given profiles
of several congressmen, describing their position on this particular issue and their record on various past issues. A scenario
describing economic conditions, and arguments for both sides
of the question would also be provided. After much debate,
a vote would be taken and a decision reached. Who wins this
simulation or game? For purposes of motivation, the designer
might build in criteria for scoring. In a case like this, the winner would probably be the player who meets his objective,

or whose plan is finally adopted by Congress. But the situation does not really have a natural or inherent winner. In an economics game, the natural winner is the player who ends up with the most money; but in a congressional debate, an intrinsic winner is not really obvious.

This observation suggests a basic difference in the use of an educational simulation and an educational game. A simulation is more likely to be applied to the study of issues rather than processes. The principal purpose of a simulation is to encourage students to express, in their own words, the basic arguments for the different sides of the issue. The principal purpose of a game, on the other hand, is to get students to make more and more intelligent decisions as they learn more about the process represented. This difference may explain why the term *simulation* is often applied to role-play games in which negotiation and debate figure prominently.

The distinction is not sharp and firm, though. If one wished to teach the procedural routes of congressional legislation, for example, a board game could be devised. Winning the game would require successful maneuvering through the committees of Congress; these could be shown graphically, with appropriate obstacles, on a gameboard. However, this emphasis on procedure could be taught in a simulation where players portrayed the same congressional entities that were represented as tokens on a gameboard. Players would put congressional bills through their paces, and negotiation and debate might play a larger part in the simulation. The key question is always, What does one wish to teach? An appropriate format for effective presentation is selected on the basis of the answer to that question, and affixing labels such as *game* or *simulation* is a mere matter of semantics.

Current Uses of Games

Serious games are currently employed for a variety of purposes beside the ones mentioned earlier. Research, planning, training, and education are activities that utilize the technique to an increasing degree.

Research

The military uses games not only for training but for research. A notable example is its investigations into the problem of insurgency, which may be defined as the clandestine and illegal activities of a group of people who seek to overthrow an established government by violence. It is a complex phenomenon that is not yet clearly understood. To investigate the ways in which insurgents seek and win support from an un-committed population, games have been designed to represent conditions similar to those identified in real-world insurgencies.

The actors in the game are the government, an initially uncommitted population, and insurgents who are at first unknown to the government. In effect, the government and insurgents represent two teams competing for the loyalty of the population. To stay in power, the government must identify the insurgents and counteract their activities. Secret police may be used as spies to search out the insurgents. The insurgents in the game must be careful not to reveal who they are; but if they are too cautious, they cannot hope to influence the population. The population is essentially passive. It is usually divided into upper, middle, and lower classes, with the latter most susceptible to the promises and persuasion of the insurgents. In the course of the game, population players undergo the cross-pressures and shifting loyalties that are presumably experienced by people in a real insurgency. Sabotage is often simulated in the game. If insurgents can muster enough arms to blow up an airport, for example, they can create chaos for the government.

At the end of each cycle of play (an ordinary day's activity), population players indicate where their loyalties lie by writing *government, insurgents,* or *neutral* on a card. The data is submitted to impartial administrators of the game, called Control. By studying the points at which loyalty shifts — and the reasons why, as revealed in numerous plays — researchers can begin to learn more about the factors contributing to insurgency. The study process does not usually end there. With more and better data, a more accurate and complicated game can then be built to test previous conclusions and to investigate fresh variables.

The accuracy of findings from this type of research depends on the soundness of the data built into the game. A game will not yield any magic solutions; nor will it correct, though it may point out, distortions built into it. Obviously, the use of research results, whether obtained from a game or from other instruments, will vary a great deal according to the sponsor's purposes.

Planning

Games have proven highly useful in the planning of complex systems. Imagine facing the task of drawing up a transportation plan for a large region of the United States. The planners designing such a system must weigh numerous considerations — technological advances in transportation, economic requirements of the region, vested political interests, limited financial resources. A game is being used to aid in this particular task. Players assume the roles of businessmen or officials of city and state governments. The business executives represent particular transportation interests, for example, trucking firms, paper companies that would stand to benefit from the expansion of one form of the transportation over another. The city and state officials also have vested interests, of course; their political life may depend on their support of one type of transportation—or perhaps on maintaining the status quo. The objective of each player is to develop a regional transportation system best suited to his interests; the scenario provides information about the region, and the player's interests are described in his profile. Players try to promote their pet plans, and vie for the support of other players. Several rounds of negotiations are played until a plan acceptable to a majority is evolved. The game thus helps planners weigh relative benefits of alternative systems; it can also reveal some specific disadvantages of any one proposal.

Education planners could profit from this type of exercise. What kinds of programs would best satisfy the needs of a particular community? Should more schools be built? Or should money be poured into remedial reading and arithmetic programs? Or into training more teachers? What, in short, is the optimum allocation of limited resources in education? A planning game, structured like the transportation one, could be developed to answer questions like these.

Training

Training games can be relatively simple. In some instances, however, the technique has been expanded into elaborate simulations. An example is the use of a simulated jungle environment in training military personnel for duty in Vietnam. Entire villages are constructed, almost exact replicas of Vietnamese ones. Geographic details, down to the flora, are reproduced, and the types of traps that can be so effectively hidden in this terrain are included. No lecture about fighting an enemy difficult to find—one who knows the the terrain infinitely better than the trainees—could be as effective as this exposure to something so very much like the real thing. The jungle props, reproducing an entire environment in minute detail, could be called the logical extension of the simulation technique.

Education

Recent years have seen a widening application of games in the educational field. The innovations range from word games for preschoolers to simulations of complex political, social, and economic processes for high school and college students. Games promise to enjoy increasing success in the classroom; they have the magnetic appeal of requiring active learning and being fun at the same time. No one suggests, however, that games and nothing else be used in a curriculum. The approach is most effective when used along with other media, not as a supplement but as an integral part of the program.

What games provide, perhaps uniquely, is the opportunity to deal with complex problems in extremely concrete ways. While the students are thus engaged, it is not essential that they know the labels for the problems and processes they are dealing with; these tags can be affixed later. The most critical phase of an educational game probably comes at the end, in the debriefing or post-play discussion. Here, the teacher can discuss with students the actions they took in the game, how effective those actions were, what errors they made, how they would alter their actions next time based on what they learned from their mistakes.

The debriefing usually yields some individualistic observations. In an experimental playing of Market, described earlier, the sixth-grader who came out with the most money was asked what he had learned in the game. The honest reply was, "Nothing." To draw him out, the game's designer asked what he had done in the game. The boy explained how he had noticed, as a storekeeper, that consumers were not buying from him because his prices were higher than his competitors'. After several cycles of play, however, the other storekeepers ran out of goods, and the consumers had to buy from him. "So I raised my prices even higher," he said, "and I made the most money."

In short, the game had allowed players to exercise the principles of supply and demand in a concrete way. Since they could talk about specific actions, events, and observations in terms of the game, the process underlying it became clear.

The use of games for teaching purposes is in a relatively early stage of development, and not all problems regarding their use have been solved. The technique will undoubtedly be refined in the future. The physical constraints of the classroom and temporal constraints of current scheduling practices may be altered to facilitate their use. Really precise evaluation procedures have yet to be developed to prove beyond an objective doubt that games, in certain circumstances, teach more effectively than other known methods. Despite the many questions remaining, games promise to become powerful educational tools; when that happens, learning may, in fact, prove to be child's play.

CHAPTER 2

WHY PLAY GAMES?

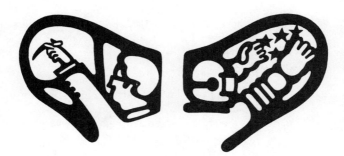

2

Games for Motivation

Games for Learning and Growth

Limitations of Games

Criteria for Game Use

Educators might well envy the seriousness and energy that children devote to play but often deny to schoolwork. That children observe the rules of a game much more conscientiously than those of the classroom is reflected in the anger and rejection directed at the child who violates the game — in contrast to the support often shown for the student who disrupts a lesson.

This is because the play world admits of no questioning, no doubt. Participation in a game necessarily implies acknowledgement of its rules. As Johan Huizinga notes in *Homo Ludens*, the play world is a magic one, a charmed circle with its own boundaries of space and time, its own rules of acceptable behavior, and a consciousness that it exists apart from the real world. Special and fragile, play is easily shattered by a call for dinner, a referee's whistle, or a spoilsport.

So powerful a spell is rarely cast by the classroom. While educators intuitively understand the child's intense involvement in play, we fail to capitalize on it much beyond kindergarten. As the child proceeds through elementary school, play is no longer used as a viable educational tool, but as a necessary recess. At best, it is a welcome break for teachers and students; at worst, it represents a bribe for students to sit out the rest of the day after letting off a little steam.

With the development of educational games, teachers can harness the energy of play for the business of school. Games increase student motivation, clarify difficult concepts and processes, help to socialize the student, and integrate classes of diverse ability levels. The author is not suggesting that games are a panacea for educational problems. They are, however, flexible enough to satisfy several educational objectives at the same time, a characteristic few media can claim. If used appropriately, the game technique can provide more rewarding experiences than many conventional methods of teaching.

What are some specific advantages — and limitations — that a teacher should expect from games? What criteria govern their use? In short, why and when should games be played in the classroom?

Games for Motivation

If educational games did nothing more than motivate students, that would be sufficient justification for playing them. The first hurdle for every teacher is apathy or resistance. Unless barriers are broken down, learning is accidental at best, and more likely nonexistent. Psychologists cite the importance of the intention to learn. Read a poem fifty times with no intent to memorize it and you will remember remarkably little. Mere exposure to material is not enough.

A variety of methods can be used to motivate students, but the most natural one is undoubtedly the best. Issues that the student perceives as directly connected to his own life hold interest for him. One would have little difficulty maintaining a lively discussion about sex in a high school class, or in an elementary class for that matter. But our educational goals extend beyond those areas that are of immediate relevance to the student. In part, it is the school's function to broaden horizons and make the world at large relevant to the individual. To accomplish this end, we must first get the student's interest.

Here educators might take a lesson from the commercial world. Packaging, or method of presentation, is a critical factor in capturing attention. Even an exciting issue can be rendered dull by inappropriate or unimaginative presentation. The concept of educational packaging does not refer merely to how attractive a textbook's cover is, or to how many full-color illustrations it has. Packaging for learning is far more complex and profound than that. It involves the selection of instructional modes and strategies tailored to particular objectives and disciplines, and encompasses the entire realm of motivation and communication.

Educational games are essentially a method of packaging concepts. Games are intrinsically motivating because the form is characterized by several dramatic features that are independent of the subject or issues dealt with. When a student listens to a lecture, participates in a discussion, or reads a textbook chapter, we assume his interest in the subject or at least his motivation to perform well in class. This premise has not proven notably valid for successful teaching and learning. When a student participates in and learns from a game, we merely assume that he shares certain basic human traits. No particular interest in the subject of a game is necessary for involvement in it. For the player, the object of a game is winning. Learning is a by-product, but motivation for further study of the topic frequently results.

Participation and Efficacy

Why are games motivating? The word *motivation* means "stimulus to action." People usually wish to act, to participate, to make things happen — in preference to being spectators, or passive creatures of events around them. Unfortunately, much of the child's school experience is of a passive nature. He is lectured to by teacher or textbook. He is assembled to do more listening. He is fire-drilled, tested, graded. It is little wonder that school can be boring and learning temporary. When outlets for a student's natural curiosity are few, the desire to explore is soon lost.

In contrast, games require active participation. Players manipulate colorful tokens, negotiate, bargain, debate, and *make decisions*. In short, they make things happen. They are the causes of events, rather than creatures of the school environment.

This is perhaps the essential characteristic that makes games motivating. The events caused by players in a game are not less real because they occur in a hypothetical world. Students gain a feeling of control over their environment. Again, the feeling of control is no less real because it is exercised over a hypothetical world. Nor does the presence of chance occurrences in a game or even unfair rules (rules that give greater advantage to one team of players over another) weaken a feeling of control over the outcome of the game. Effectiveness and control are not synonymous with success and winning. A player who makes a poor decision in a game nevertheless perceives his impact on the game environment.

The sense of efficacy that games permit and encourage is not only an underlying reason for their motivational power, but an important educational benefit. In a world so large and complex, few individuals feel capable of affecting their environment. A sense of powerlessness leads to apathy and general malaise, a condition that reinforces its source. Students quickly learn that the complex school environment in which they operate is beyond their control. They retreat. A host of defense mechanisms is deployed, and the defeatist attitude persists beyond the school years.

Educational games provide the student with a scaled-down model of the world over which he can exert influence and control. They can serve as a partial antidote to the passivity that the typical school environment tends to create or reinforce.

Intrinsic and Prompt Feedback

Not only do game participants cause events; they know immediately what they have done. When a player makes a decision in a game, it has immediate effect. He fares well or poorly. Other players respond to his decision. If he pays too high a price for a purchase in an economics game, his financial resources are quickly diminished. If he agrees to vote for a certain candidate early in an election game, he may discover that he has yielded his bargaining power too soon. He takes action and learns the consequences. He does not have to wait for a test to be graded or for a teacher to approve or correct his verbal response.

Educators agree that quick feedback is a valuable reinforcement of learning. The growth of programmed instruction was one manifestation of this belief. Yet in many classroom activities, students find that feedback on their performance is slow or perhaps unavailable, incomplete, and largely artificial. Few teachers would be able to react to all students in any complete and satisfying fashion. For example, an idea contributed by a student in discussion can receive only brief attention from the class. A creative, somewhat offbeat idea is frequently dismissed or ignored when, in fact, fuller attention to it would reveal a clever point. When feedback is slow or absent, its impact is lost. The student is no longer interested. But a ratio of one teacher to thirty students makes the situation difficult to improve.

More crucial is the quality of feedback the student usually receives. It is artificial. It comes in the form of a good grade on a test, or an answer that matches a textbook key. In short, it is externally imposed and rarely explained.

In a game, feedback is not only prompt but natural. The player knows the reason for his success or failure. Good strategy works. He wins money, or gets elected, or gets his plan accepted. His actions and decisions are judged or reinforced along the same lines on which they were made. He is not asked to believe on faith that the teacher knows better or that the answers in the back of his textbook are infallible. Right and wrong are not simply handed down from above. Ironically, the hypothetical world of a game reflects the feedback process of the real world more accurately than does the customary operation of the classroom.

Goal-direction and Closure

Not only are games active and responsive, they are goal-directed. The objective of winning is initially a powerful motivating force. Observation has revealed that by the time a classroom game is finished, most children do not care whether they have won or lost. Nevertheless, the game is not considered officially over until it has been scored to determine the winner or winners.

A similar sense of closure is lacking in most conventional media. The end of a textbook chapter gives some degree of closure, but the student may look forward to no greater reward than a test. Unless he is interested in the subject, there is little intrinsic motivation for him to finish the chapter. It will only be followed by more of the same.

In contrast, a game has well-defined limits and obvious closure. This does not mean that all games have a natural end. If a game focuses on an election, or on getting consensus on a plan to reduce pollution, for example, the game ends when such conditions have been achieved. Many games, however, end after a given time period rather than at a climax. Nevertheless, until that point, players are working toward the objective of winning within the stated rules of play. Because the activity is highly structured and the objectives are clear, motivation is enhanced. A natural by-product of intense involvement in goal-directed activity is the extension of attention span. While a game should not be overly long, students can easily sustain interest for the three to five classroom periods usually required.

Uncertainty and Open-endedness

While the goals or objectives of a game are clear, the outcome is not. Nobody knows who the winner will be or what events are likely to occur during play. The same game may be played repeatedly, with an entirely different pattern of interaction and resolution each time. For children, there is nothing terribly uncomfortable about this atmosphere of uncertainty. On the contrary, uncertainty lends an element of drama to play. The student knows the textbook is going to provide him with "the answers" if only he pays proper attention. In a game the player knows he will have some influence on the outcome, but the actions of other players, as well as elements of chance, operate beyond his effective control to determine the ultimate result.

Further, there is rarely a "correct" outcome to a game. Obviously, in a game focusing on a political election, the outcome is neither correct nor incorrect; it is simply more satisfactory to some participants than to others. In games focusing on a community problem, such as controlling pollution, the outcome may be more or less successful but it cannot be incorrect. This flexibility or open-endedness frees the student from inhibitions about being wrong, and encourages creative play and experimentation.

Open-endedness represents both a reason why games are motivating and a benefit from their use. Students readily accept degrees of ambiguity. Particularly as they get older, the complexities of the real world and the absence of easy black or white answers become apparent. Classroom learning tends not to keep pace with the student's growing awareness. As a result, the discrepancy between the world presented in school and the real world outside increases, contributing to youthful cynicism regarding the credibility of the school system.

As open-end activities, educational games inject realism into learning situations and allow leeway for experimentation and creativity on the part of students. Both attributes are essential in the classroom if we are sincere about preparing students for adult life in the real world.

Reality, Relevance, and Role Imitation

The introduction of a greater degree of reality into the classroom has a potent motivational effect on students. Educational games usually focus on real-world problems, although this need not be so. A game focuses on whatever the designers select, and card games, for example, require the manipulation of abstract symbols only. Nevertheless, most games reflect grown-up activities and roles. For that reason, they have great appeal to youngsters. Children love to imitate. They relish the opportunity to engage in activities that are usually associated with adults only. By providing the opportunity to imitate roles, games capitalize on a natural tendency and direct it toward educational goals.

One could argue that *independent of the subject*, game learning tends to have closer connections to students' lives than many conventional classroom activities. The operational characteristic of games (decision making in the context of roles) makes them more realistic and relevant to students than, for example, a textbook chapter about a statesman's dilemma in deciding on war or peace. Because the student must make the decision himself, the factors to be considered take on greater importance.

This is true even in games with fictitious backdrops, such as those involving relations among hypothetical countries. The use of hypothetical settings is merely a convenience; it is a way of treating basic principles and issues without the necessity of exactly simulating a particular situation. Where the specifics of a situation are not part of the teaching objective, a fictional setting also helps to avoid the preconceptions students might have about a specific case.

History games, too, usually seem more concrete than history books. The decisions players must make in history games usually involve timeless problems faced by society. Even in a game about eighteenth century Anglo-American colonial relations, students confront the modern problems of accepting or defying authority, or enforcing governmental authority with political finesse. Even in a game about the post–Civil War period, students face the still current issues of unequal distribution of economic and political power, the role of government in society, the problems of an oppressed minority. Only the rules of the game constrain the players so that the actions they can take reflect the attitudes and limitations of a different era. The point need not be labored. It is simply worth noting that having to face a crucial decision in a game can make a historical issue extremely relevant and concrete to the student.

Interaction and Peer Learning

Because games utilize interests that normally compete with school work for the child's attention, motivation is increased. As any teacher knows, children are social beings who love to talk with peers. And their bodies apparently contain more energy than can be expended by just sitting in class; it comes as no surprise that restlessness is a feature of most classes. Almost all educational games, however, call for interaction among players—permitting or even requiring physical movement around a gameboard or the classroom. The opportunity to use up energy and satisfy the desire to communicate is thus integral to the learning experience. In games, what would normally be distractions are redirected to educational ends.

Even more valuable is the impact of peer interaction. Children learn from their peers, and probably learn more in this way than they do from their teachers. Educators are becoming increasingly aware of this relationship, and observations of peer interaction have given rise to experiments in peer teaching. In some school systems, students are being coached to teach their peers or younger students.

Structured peer interactions constitute a fundamental attribute of educational games. Also, teamwork requires that the informal exchanges between students during play be directed to game issues and strategies. In few other classroom activities is peer interaction encouraged. In fact, this natural channel for learning is often viewed as disruptive (talking in class) or dishonest (cheating), and is frowned on. In games, peer interaction is harnessed for specific educational goals.

Competition and Cooperation

All games are competitive to some extent. So are most people. Educational games thus exploit the inclination to compete and channel it for educational purposes. One has only to recall the time-honored and pervasive institution of the spelling bee to note how effective competitive exercises can be. By introducing the element of competition, teachers have long been able to motivate students to go through an otherwise dull, mechanical process. Spelling was an obvious candidate for animation with, fortunately, a simple solution. For more sophisticated and, one might argue, more significant subjects, educational games can tap the same competitive instinct and thus increase motivation to learn. The Nova schools in Florida have done just that by developing an academic Olympics around a series of educational games.

Cooperation is a strong element of the very games that are competitive. Players on one team cooperate among themselves to compete with other teams. In games designed for individual roles rather than for teams, alliances are almost always necessary for winning. Games thus tap the human instinct to cooperate, even to conspire—in contrast to most conventional classroom activities, which demand individual performance and frequently penalize cooperation.

Position and Self-image

A few leaders, if not heroes, emerge from most classes. The other students come to expect the chosen few to give the brightest answers, write the best papers, and receive the highest grades. These "others" do not hope to achieve the same degree of success as the elite; nor do they expect to receive as much of the teacher's, and perhaps their peers', approbation. Eventually, limited expectations of success produce or reinforce limited efforts. Educational games provide fresh opportunities for "the others." In a game, there is no guarantee that "the best" students will win. There is no monopolizing of activity by "the best," since everybody participates at the same time. While the system behind the conventional operation of a classroom has been successfully internalized by the leaders, no such system operates in a game. A combination of good decisions and good luck is required to win a game. The rewards do not depend on conformity to a teacher's rules of procedure, nor is there one right way of arriving at one right answer. Unorthodox, imaginative solutions are just as good and sometimes better than conventional ones. Verbal skills, which are critical in conventional activities, are often subordinate in game situations; social skills are sometimes more important in games than they are in the more usual classroom activities. Also, games are not graded in the way that other activities are; while this may present problems for the teacher, it removes inhibitions for the student. Games also offer more leadership roles than are normally available in other classroom activities. Students quickly perceive these differences, and can devote their attention to the activity at hand without worrying about the cues and signals, the penalties and rewards that usually demand attention. It is only a game, and they cannot lose much.

Magic

Games are different not only from ordinary classroom activities but from all real-world activities. That is not to say that games do not treat real problems and situations. They do. But for the players, the game situation is admittedly make-believe. The roles they play and the decisions they make are different from their functions in the real world. While many adults observe the world of make-believe only passively in such forms as movies and the theatre, children create make-believe worlds all the time. The younger they are, the more they imitate. They play house. They play school. They play cowboys and Indians. They imitate anything they have become acquainted with in the course of their short lives. And they do it voluntarily and enthusiastically.

Play is so fundamental in all cultures that it would be a formidable task indeed to analyze its origin, significance, or raison d'être.[1] Fortunately, it isn't necessary to dissect play before taking advantage of its motivational possibilities. The inclination to play is a natural urge, one that should be exploited by the teacher who is seeking to stimulate his students' desire to learn.

Games for Learning and Growth

Facts are currently out of fashion. How many times have we heard it said that students must learn concepts; they can always pick up the facts later. As a reaction against the old-fashioned notion that education's job was to drill some basic facts about grammar and history, science and math into every head, the current fashion has served its purpose. Like most reactions, it has gone a bit too far and is swinging back to a more viable synthesis of the two extreme views.

One manifestation of the reaction against facts was the reaction against textbooks. While these will never be wholly out of fashion, the recognition that textbooks are not sufficient to teach everything has been salutary. In science, math, and writing, the need for active exercises has long

---

[1] The ambitious should see J. Huizinga, *Homo Ludens* (Boston: Beacon Press, 1955) for an analysis of the role of play in society.

been realized and fulfilled. In the social sciences, however, passive instructional modes are still used, and it is here that animation is most needed and most difficult to achieve. Our goals extend beyond conveying information, but our methods lag behind. Educational games can be profitably used in any subject area; but they promise to be most important in the social sciences, to provide laboratory experiences that are otherwise difficult to create.

Educational games are in part, a product of the reaction against facts — the reaction against gearing instruction to the acquisition and storage of raw, unused, and sometimes unusable data. The primary educational objectives of games do not emphasize the acquisition of facts by the players. Rather, games are usually concerned with developing problem-solving abilities and with cultivating an understanding of the processes. The game package makes it particularly well suited to the area of applied knowledge. Because games emphasize decision making, players must utilize what they know—facts, concepts, intuitive judgments —and apply it to the problem at hand. Games thus tend to function best as situations for teaching processes and problem solving. They are less efficient when applied simply to teaching facts, the raw data on which thought and action are based.

It must be emphasized, however, that the educational objectives of a game are determined by the designers, and a game can be designed simply to convey information. In fact, educational games for simple drill—arithmetic operations, vocabulary, names, places, dates—have been designed and used with success. Strictly speaking, these games are not simulations of processes. Rather, they are vehicles for conveying information; they exploit the game's motivational or "fun" attributes more than its cognitive potential.

Information from Games

It should not be assumed that information is not conveyed in educational games, though it may appear in unorthodox form. Facts are the basic material from which a game is built. Take that most fact-ridden discipline, history. One experimental game is designed to teach not only the process of revolution in general, but the specific causes of the English Civil War. The game takes the form of role playing in which each player represents a real historical character, as described in a profile. Most players are prominent country gentlemen and Members of Parliament who are Puritan and devoted to the constitutional rights of Englishmen. A small number play royal advisers and sympathizers, and one portrays Charles I himself. Players are informed that Parliament has been dissolved by the king, who is attempting to rule without it. Unknown to the players is the fact that two teams exist, each with different rules. The royalist group has the objective of obtaining revenue (a specific sum) each cycle. The parliamentary actors have the objective of making as much money as possible, and resisting what they believe are illegal methods of taxation. The basic course of action for the royalist group is to impose taxes and to control religious beliefs. The basic course of action for the parliamentary group is to invest in trading companies, and to respond to the royalists' attempts at taxation and religious control. Contingencies, such as the trial of John Hampden, are introduced at various points in the game through the device of news bulletins. The final bulletin announces the invasion of the Scots, who demand a large sum of money from King Charles. The game is rigged to make it impossible for Charles to raise the money without calling Parliament, at which point the population has the opportunity to demand redress of grievances before assenting to taxation.

The game conveys information in several vivid ways—the profiles give detailed portraits of individual characters; the news bulletins describe specific events of the period; the roles and rules introduce such institutions as Parliament and monarchy. These are the minimum items of information one should expect a student to acquire. But if that is all he learns, the game has probably not been worth playing. It would be quicker and easier to give students the equivalent of a few profiles and news bulletins to read at home. What we want students to do through the game is to become aware of two existing views of the issues; to understand the social, religious, economic, and political aspects of the conflict; to analyze the possible resolutions of the conflict as well as the specific historical one; to generalize the factors in the conflict and apply the generalizations to other cases. This is a big order, but one better filled by the game than by a text or lecture.

Comprehension

To play a game the student must understand his function in a situation. If he is a consumer in an economics game, he has money with which to buy commodities. If he is a Member of Parliament in a historical simulation, he must oppose taxes levied without his consent. In performing his role, he must interact with other players. As a result, comprehension of his function in relation to others is deepened. He negotiates with retailers or tax collectors, and in so doing acquires an understanding of their roles. Much of his activity is spontaneous. As situations arise in the course of play, he must respond;

often, he does so on the basis of limited information. If a retailer raises his prices, the consumer knows only that he wants to get the most and best goods for his money. He must make the decision either to play the higher price, bargain for a lower price, do without the commodity, or try to buy it elsewhere. The decision is often arbitrary in the first stages of play; but as he recognizes the consequences of earlier decisions, the player begins to consider the likely results of alternative decisions he might make.

Analysis and Synthesis

In considering possible courses of action, the player analyzes the relationships among the assorted facts at his disposal. If he pays a higher price for a commodity, he will have less money. If he doesn't, he will not obtain a presumably beneficial or necessary item. A salutary effect of the analytic process is the discovery that not all the answers are immediately available. If he seeks to buy the desired item elsewhere, he may not find it, or the price may be higher still, and he risks losing the opportunity to buy from the first retailer if he decides to shop around. The corollary to analysis is the synthesis of a plan of action. In a game, a considered decision represents the development of a plan. This can be quite sophisticated. If the player notices that prices are best in stores that are least crowded, he may develop a hypothesis—one we would call the principle of supply and demand.

Judgment

Teachers often have to cajole, pressure, and implore students to make judgments about written materials. Is it accurate? Biased? Logical? Is the solution effective? In playing a game, students implicitly evaluate their own actions and those of other players continuously. Good tactics or strategy are rewarded by success in the game. A player quickly discovers if his tactics are effective. If they are not, he is led to evaluate what he did wrong, and to find ways to improve his strategy. When a game depends heavily on negotiation, he must evaluate the deals or promises offered by other players in terms of how well these satisfy his own interests and how honest the other players are. This kind of judgment is often more significant than the attempt to find the flaw in an argument or to name a particular quality in a piece of writing.

Verbal and Interpersonal Skills

Because most games require negotiation and compromise, verbal and interpersonal skills are developed. Arguments must be gathered and presented persuasively. Players must learn when to yield and compromise, and when to hold out for their own interests. In the play of a game simulating the Korean War, one student took such an aggressive action that he precipitated World War III — to the horror and anger of the other players. In a second play of the game with the same students, the aggressive fellow was much more subdued. While games will not necessarily produce diplomats and pacifists, they do require attention to the relation between behaving acceptably and securing one's own interests. They also stimulate players to find the most appropriate methods of getting what they want. If a player is a racketeer trying to secure the loyalty of tough city kids, he will not use the same manner as someone playing a legislator trying to get his pet project passed. Games thus sharpen one's perceptions of other people, and develop the ability to evaluate and respond to their needs and interests.

Flexibility

Flexibility is an intellectual habit as well as an attitude. Educational games cultivate a flexible approach to problems because there is no single correct outcome nor is there one best strategy that will always work. Games investigate dynamic processes in which many variables operate at the same time, and experimentation with solutions is encouraged. This approach encourages initiative and risk taking, realism and imagination. Ultimately, it can be an antidote to the cynicism often produced by the handing down of "right answers" that are found to have little relation to the real world.

Transfer or Application

Games encourage flexibility and experimentation. As an outgrowth, they nurture an intellectual approach that can be applied to problems other than the issues presented in the games. Standard exercises that attempt to get students to apply what they have learned to a slightly new situation, rely mainly on the transfer of concepts. When a student has learned how to add apples and oranges, he is expected to be able to add pears and bananas as well. But after a student has played a game about a particular revolution, he should be able to do more than understand and analyze the causes of a different uprising; he should be able to explain other related phenomena such as a failure or absence of revolution in a culture, the causes of urban riots or a rural insurgency. Not enough empirical evidence is available yet for judging the transferability of knowledge and skills learned from games. However, one might assume that the exercise of analytic skills in games should cultivate the habit of analysis in other situations.

Problem Solving

Games are particularly well suited to develop the problem-solving abilities of students. The objective of the game may be to teach the process of revolution, the laws of supply and demand, the meaning of civil rights, the problem of pollution, the development of an urban area, the reasons for the Industrial Revolution, the operation of subtraction, or the source of shadows. Whatever the issue may be, it is presented in the form of a problem that the player must contribute to solving. Many abilities are called into use in the game—the student must have his wits about him. These needed skills might be analytic, mathematical, or for that matter, intuitive. Once a solution has been achieved, or the game completed, the steps used in reaching it can be reviewed and analyzed. Chapter 1 cited the example of a child who, as storekeeper in an economics game, noticed that nobody would buy his goods because his prices were higher than those of his competitors. When the other storekeepers ran out of goods, however, consumers had to buy from him. He proceeded to raise his prices and make the most money. The child who accidentally or instinctively acted this way in the game no doubt learned more about supply and demand than had he dutifully recited the principle as stated in a textbook. He had discovered it himself in a limited and concrete problem situation, and the experience should improve his ability to handle a new and different problem.

Socialization

Implicit in the preceding discussion are the social benefits of using games as a teaching device. For example, the respect children normally show for the rules of a game may facilitate cultivation of respect for the rules of the classroom, school, and society. Students who find pleasure in flaunting the rules of school and society do not seem to behave that way in game situations. This is not to suggest that games be used simply as convenient tools for enforcing conformity. They do, however, provide students with an opportunity to empathize with roles and positions that they find unfamiliar or perhaps view with hostility. In this way, games help to broaden the student's understanding of other viewpoints and attitudes.

Games can be especially beneficial to students who are ordinarily shy and withdrawn; they seem to lose inhibitions and behave in surprisingly active and communicative ways during play. Because normal relationships are suspended and real-world threats removed, the risk of losing face is lessened, and students participate freely. This is not universally true, certainly, but observation suggests that games encourage and elicit active behavior in children who are otherwise passive in class. In part, this heightened activity can be attributed to the suspension of the usual classroom evaluation system — it is difficult to grade a student's performance in a game. Inhibitions created by the fear of being wrong or of receiving a poor grade are removed and freer participation is encouraged.

Active behavior, however, is not entirely explained by the suspension of ordinary classroom constraints since the same phenomenon is encountered in game play with adults. Mistakes, exposure of ignorance, unacceptable behavior — situations normally avoided — can be tolerated because they may be excused as creations or blunders of the fictitious character rather than of the individual himself. Exploration and experimentation with new behavior patterns is thus made possible in an unthreatening environment.

Peer relationships are also cultivated by game playing. Since games usually depend heavily on personal interactions, students learn the limits of acceptable behavior among their peers. They do this, of course, outside of school. And they normally do it in a peculiar context within the classroom (for example, outstanding academic achievement frequently falls outside the peer definition of acceptable behavior). Instead of ignoring or discouraging peer-group behavior patterns, games relate them to legitimate learning situations.

Educational games can add depth to the socialization process in the classroom. Game situations emphasize interpersonal relations; they encourage self-restraint and attention to the needs of other individuals; and they do so in relation to serious, real-world problems. Socialization in games often occurs in the context of adult predicaments and roles, which become increasingly meaningful to the students. This is yet another way in which games help reduce the gap between classroom activities and the world outside.

Limitations of Games

By no means do games represent a solution to our myriad educational problems. They are a new technique and a promising one. Their unique characteristics can facilitate the achievement of educational goals that conventional media fail to fulfill. But like any technique or methodology, they must be used appropriately to gain what advantages they offer. Overuse or misuse will otherwise place them, like many other techniques, in the graveyard of educational fads.

Games can accomplish some tasks better than others, and the teacher needs to discriminate. Also a number of questions about their effects have been raised, suggesting qualifications on their use. Definite answers are yet to be found to these questions. For the present, the teacher must rely heavily on subjective judgment in assessing the value of using a particular game with his class.

Can Games Be Too Motivating?

Intense involvement in educational games usually enhances learning for the student. But it is possible that involvement can become too intense. Most games are not zero-sum games where one person wins and everybody else loses. Very often there are several winners or different degrees of winning. As in real-world situations, winning and losing are not clear-cut and mutually exclusive categories. In some games, however — where an election is simulated, for example — the losers may be intensely disappointed. In a game like Revolution, where the country gentlemen are supposed to become frustrated because they have no channels for controlling the king, players may become overly emotional. Ordinarily, students understand that "it's only a game," even when they discover during play that the game is rigged against a particular team. Some question may arise about the wisdom of trying to produce anger and frustration in students. As yet, there is not enough empirical evidence to judge the value or danger of doing so. But one point seems obvious: Students resent being shielded from the realities of the world. Perhaps having students experience anger at being treated unfairly can increase their empathy with people in similar real-world situations. At the very least, discussion of the matter would be an attempt to deal rationally with the kind of irrationality that happens all the time in the real world.

The Question of Simplification

In developing any instructional materials, selection and simplification are necessary. The medium dictates, in part, the kind of simplification that must be made. In a textbook, the author is forced to describe simultaneous events in a sequential order. In a game, not every aspect of a problem can be handled, and abstract ideas must be represented concretely. If commodities are being traded, the number of goods must be limited to prevent chaos and the prices perhaps adjusted so that the sums can be handled in the game. In a historical game, time has to be condensed and events presented as if they occurred close upon each other. Girls may be asked to play male roles. Power may be represented by plastic chips. If players are trading goods across the ocean, the designer has the choice of requiring many moves to cross, thereby simulating time, or ignoring the time element in the interest of preventing boredom. Also, variations of the basic process being described by the game usually must be omitted.

Nevertheless, educational games permit relatively sophisticated treatment of the issues under investigation. The effect of many things happening simultaneously can be built into the game; so can the inability of any individual to perceive everything that is operating—hence the necessity of making decisions on the basis of limited information. When the player learns the rules of the game, he acquires a basic understanding of the simulated process. Exceptions and qualifications can be postponed until the discussion that follows the game.

Do Games Teach the "Wrong" Values?

In game situations, players assume roles that frequently require behavior we do not condone. In a history game about the expansion of the American West, for example, players buy and sell slaves as a matter of course. In a game dealing with the Industrial Revolution in England, players compete to amass wealth; to succeed, entrepreneurs pay the lowest possible wages to workers. In a game set in the Reconstruction period of American history, the distribution of power between ex-slaves and plantation owners is grossly unfair and plantation owners are encouraged, through the rules of the game, to exercise their power purely for their own advantage.

These situations require behavior that would be explicitly discouraged and condemned in class. Does a game requiring such behavior, then, teach that behavior? By permitting students to exercise such behavior, does a game, by implication, condone it?

In the author's opinion, it does not. A game is essentially value free; it does not intrinsically condone or condemn any set of values or behavior. In all of the examples above, the game structures an environment in which particular behavior patterns are acceptable. In so doing, the game in no way suggests that such behavior is moral, effective, or appropriate to any set of circumstances outside the game—or even that it was moral in the situation represented by the game.

The concern over values portrayed in a game derives in part from the basic puritanical bent of our school systems. We dislike confronting the world as it really is, or as it was. When corrupt or immoral behavior is studied, it must be condemned as such. In games, however, study consists of "acting out." Opportunity to evaluate or to condemn is delayed. There is an implicit fear among some educators that the actual practice or exercise of "immoral" behavior will be internalized automatically by the student. In discussion, one can always stay on the "right" side of an issue; in a game, some players will represent the "wrong" side.

Further, text and game treatment of a subject tend to differ in emphasis. For example, while few objections are raised to studying the Industrial Revolution in textbooks, some concern has been expressed over playing a game about it. Typical textbook studies of the Industrial Revolution focus on the technological advances, the economic organization, and the resulting overall improvement in the material quality of life. While there is no typical game treatment of the Industrial Revolution, one such game examines the relation between industrialists, workers, and farmers; in simulating the flow of goods, jobs, and money, human relations and inequalities of power and money are the prominent issues. In this example, the game leads to questions of power and justice in relation to the student's concrete experience. The realities of this situation are disturbing and uncomfortable to some educators; even the fact that students handle play money in class has been a source of some concern.

The desire to keep the world pure for the young student is an untenable habit with the teachers of today's generation. A realistic study of a range of human behavior is far more likely to produce critical, rational thinkers than the isolationist approach. And the opportunity to analyze and evaluate actions and attitudes actually experienced in class ought not to be forfeited.

Does a Game Depend on What Students Already Know?

Most games, whether or not they utilize gameboards and other paraphernalia, require some degree of role playing. To that extent, they may require the student to act out ways of behaving and thinking that are strange to him. In a game about industrialization, for example, entrepreneurs must attempt to pay the lowest possible wages to workers. Such calculating, self-interested behavior is alien to many students. In a game about the English Civil War, some players are asked to defend their religious principles against royal attack. Few students have ever experienced an attack upon their religious or other principles, and the specific Puritan position is abstract and unfamiliar to them. In an American history game about the Continental Congress, the gradual evolution of and growing commitment to the idea of independence is simulated. The fact that independence represented treason against the king, and therefore a momentous decision for the delegates, is difficult for twentieth century students to comprehend. And in games specifically designed to cultivate interpersonal skills — such as interview behavior, persuasiveness, or perceptiveness

—we are asking the student to act out the very behavior we are trying to teach him.

The question then arises whether such games can accomplish their objectives unless the student has adequate pre-existing knowledge and experience of the subject or skills involved. How much must the student bring to a game in order to learn from it? If a student's experience is critical to the game's success, does he really learn from it at all? These questions express the reverse of the concern as to whether games can teach the "wrong" values.

In each game, the rules and profiles delineating the attitudes of the actors are designed to elicit the behavior required to learn the process or issue under study. A well-constructed profile includes specific responses that a player is expected to make as encounters with other players and outside events occur. In a job-interview game, the interviewer's profile may tell him that poor posture and gum chewing are habits he cannot tolerate in a receptionist for his company. An applicant in the game may be described as having these habits. In the encounter between the two, both applicant and interviewer learn the negative effects of such habits when the interviewer follows his profile and does not hire the applicant.

In a history game about the Continental Congress, delegates, although they do not know it initially, fall into three categories: radical, moderate, and conservative. Each delegate is told in his profile that he has supported the various forms of colonial protest to that date. However, each is given a different degree of willingness to carry protest further. This is clearly spelled out: "You will support a movement to end all trade with Britain but will not support armed resistance." "You believe that a break with Britain is the only means of securing colonial liberty and are concerned that many delegates are willing to sacrifice some colonial liberties for the sake of reconciliation." As further acts of protest are discussed according to game agenda, players respond as instructed in their profiles and in letters they receive.

In the game about the Industrial Revolution, entrepreneurs who pay high wages lose the game. What constitutes high wages is not always immediately obvious to the player in the course of play. But he discovers whether his decisions have been inappropriate to his role when their consequences are revealed.

A game that is structured tightly enough controls the interactions between players, and between players and rules, so that straightforward adherence to the profiles and rules will produce adequate results in the game. Win or lose, the entrepreneur will learn the relationship between his allocation of resources and his financial success. The delegates to the Continental Congress will learn the spectrum of colonial opinion toward Britain, the gradual polarization of moderate delegates to radical or conservative points of view as the conflict heightens, and the reasons that some delegates refused the final treasonable step.

Almost all games begin slowly, for players require some time to become familiar with rules and roles. In the Industrial Revolution game, players will initially perform the operations of the game (hire workers, produce cloth, collect income, pay wages, and so forth) in a rather mechanical fashion; as the game proceeds, they will play with more strategy. In role-play games, interaction is noticeably briefer and less active at the outset than at the later stages when players become more familiar with their own roles and are stimulated by the ideas and arguments of other players.

A student need not be thoroughly familiar with a role or a situation to play a game. For example, concern over whether an affluent student can assume the part of a poor, oppressed actor in a game is unwarranted. The rules of such a game will give the student fewer resources and privileges relative to other players or to his objectives; even if he has never felt deprived before, the player will feel deprived in the context of the game.

Nevertheless, the personality and previous experience of a student *is* an important input to a game's operation. The more vocal, aggressive student will play his role more convincingly. The more calculating student will probably make a better entrepreneur in a game than the student who can be easily persuaded to pay higher wages. For this reason, casting the roles is sometimes suggested, particularly if a game has a few leadership roles whose active play is important to the momentum of the game. Since games are interactive, convincing play on the part of some players helps to stimulate those who are less certain of their roles.

On a broader scale, however, certain concepts are so alien to the twentieth century student that a role-play game would probably not be the most effective approach to the subject. Take the essentially medieval idea that "the king can do no wrong." This fiction, still maintained in the eighteenth century, was the basis on which American colonial protests against Britain were directed against the king's "evil ministers." It explains, too, why Thomas Paine's *Common Sense,* attacking monarchy directly, was a bold statement at the time. A game built around this concept of kingship would probably be very difficult to construct because little in the student's experience could be tapped or applied to the situation. This does not mean that the concept could not be included in a game with broader focus; but a role-play game, aimed primarily at conveying this concept, would probably be inefficient.

Input Versus Output

What do games teach? There is no simple answer to this broad and crucial question, and little conclusive research has been done. (See Chapter 5 for further discussion.) Among individuals familiar with educational games, however, the observation is often made that games seem to teach broad skills and approaches—negotiation, rhetoric, the habits of weighing costs and benefits in decision making—rather than specific concepts. On the other hand, many proponents of educational games assert that a player learns from a game only what has been built into it.

The two contentions seem incompatible, yet both are correct. If a game teaches only what has been built into it, it is because the designer selects the emphasis and constructs the game accordingly. Thus a game could teach the detailed procedural operation of Congress rather than the negotiating and bargaining aspects of the legislative process. But games are not intrinsically limited to teaching overall skills such as negotiating. History games are particularly good testimony to this fact. A number of games have been constructed to teach specific historical concepts and processes—the operation of mercantilist trade, for example, or the relation between social classes in the South after the Civil War; such games do not depend heavily on negotiating or on cost-benefit analysis, nor is it their primary objective to teach those skills.

On the other hand, games represent perhaps the only medium that can give the student practice in decision making, negotiating, and other complex skills. Educational games on topics such as Congress, war, and labor-management relations therefore tend to emphasize those facets of the institutions or processes that are inadequately treated or basically difficult to teach through other media. Games are particularly well suited for teaching broad skills, and designers have taken advantage of that property. It should not be assumed, however, that all games must emphasize those skills.

Criteria for Game Use

The technique of cost effectiveness is popular in government and industry. In brief, it is a method of analyzing value gained for time and money expended, making it possible to evaluate alternative decisions before limited resources have been wasted. The woman who spends forty cents on carfare to save two cents on milk knows nothing of this approach. Surprising answers are sometimes obtained; for instance, building more and better highways could, in a given situation, be expected to save more lives than investing more money in medical research.

To some extent, most people implicitly make decisions on this basis. The woman who decides that it is more effective for her to work and hire a housekeeper — taking into account her interests, talents, and financial needs or desires — has figured out that one course of action is more cost-effective for her than another. Teachers do, or should do, the same thing in selecting educational materials. For every classroom activity, there is an investment required and learning expected. More time for less learning is obviously undesirable.

In deciding to use a game over other media in a particular instance, the time required and the expected benefits must be weighed before an intelligent choice can be made. Obviously, such a decision must be made on the basis of imperfect information, since expected benefits can only be predicted. For discussion purposes, let us assume that effective learning is the prime objective, with other goals being constant. Remember, too, that games require more classroom time than most conventional materials. Three classroom periods are probably the minimum necessary for briefing, playing, and debriefing or discussion after the game. Some games are designed to last for five or six periods; often they consume that much time despite expectations. Though games can be designed and used to teach almost anything, it would be wasteful to employ them indiscriminately. The specific criteria for using games take into account, of course, their previously discussed limitations.

Games to Motivate

Novel and visually exciting, games have tremendous motivational appeal. This is a fundamental reason for using games, particularly if one accepts the premise that unless students can be interested in a subject and motivated to learn about it, the classroom time spent on that subject will be largely ineffective. Once students have been involved in a subject through playing a game, they can be expected to remain interested even when the game is followed by conventional materials.

Essentially, the teacher faces the choice of spending, say a week on a textbook chapter about supply and demand, or about two weeks on the same subject using a game and a text. Not only will unmotivated students become interested, but they will learn the basic principles from the game; this will heighten their interest in the text, and make the issues discussed there more understandable and salient. Merely plodding through the material in one week, in contrast, would be of little value.

Many social studies topics are viewed with little enthusiasm by students. How unfortunate that is, when social studies should be of prime interest to them because it deals with the business of living. Part of the problem is that dynamic processes are dissected and presented sequentially in dry text. One of the most exiting phenomena in American political life is the process of legislating, for example. But what most students get is a step-by-step description of how a bill becomes a law. The exciting, suspenseful heart of the matter is usually ignored in favor of the legal, procedural aspects. Not all bills are interesting, but take vital issues that affect people directly, such as an increase in taxes, a change in conscription laws, or federal expenditure for highways. Build these issues, the procedure, the personalities, and the politics into a game. Students can play the role of legislators—negotiating, making deals, facing reelection—and in so doing, they can learn the human factors, the constraints of limited resources, as well as the steps required for a bill to become a law. Text descriptions can then serve as an aid to debriefing the game and summarizing the process.

In almost any situation where students are not already motivated to learn, educational games serve as useful springboards for further study. If a teacher is reasonably assured that students will learn from a game itself, and will then be more likely to pursue the subject through other media, the time invested in game play is well spent.

Some games are designed primarily for motivational purposes. One set of mathematics games has been designed for students who have had difficulty learning arithmetic operations. These games do not teach more sophisticated processes than a set of math exercises might. But they do provide a way for students to get practice in addition, subtraction, and other operations without the drudgery of writing out numerous workbook exercises. For students who do not need such drill, classroom time need not be devoted to these games.

Similarly, although games are not best or uniquely suited to teach facts, they can be profitably used for this purpose when students are unmotivated. The most efficient way to teach a single fact—that Columbus discovered America in 1492, for example—would be to say so. But simple games could be quite effective for teaching a set of facts—for example, important discoveries in the age of exploration, major technological advances in the first industrial revolution, the valences of elements and the configuration of compounds in chemistry. If a teacher believes that students will work more adeptly with chemical formulas if they memorize valence numbers, he can construct a simple card game, resembling the common game of "war," in which cards with higher numbers capture those with lower numbers. Such an approach could motivate students to learn what would be dull to study in conventional form.

Games to Teach Complex Problems

Often a game can clarify a complex issue or process that students are having difficulty grasping. This is not because the game distorts the process and omits aspects of it, but because it requires each student to focus on only a limited part of it. Each player has a specific role, with specific functions or activities that he is asked to perform. In a game on legislation, each player is one legislator with limited interests. He encounters other interests, both in alliance and in conflict with his own, in the form of other individuals. The rules of the game require that he move through stated channels. No one student is likely to see the overall process while playing. Synthesis of the entire process is the function of the debriefing, when each student reviews his own experience and contributes his perceptions of what occurred during play.

In a game about the pollution problem, the economic, social, political, and technological factors are embodied in individual roles. Each student must consider all these sides of the problem in a limited but integrated way. During negotiations, as individuals come into conflict, each constraint on controlling pollution is expanded and fleshed out as students state their own views. Students learn where pollution comes from; who it hurts most; who has the most money in a community; who is willing to spend most to control pollution; what technological devices are available and how expensive and effective they are; what political interests support abatement or oppose it; how difficult it is to achieve compromise; and the short- and long-term consequences of not controlling pollution. All this in elementary school!

Also, many of the processes that students find complex are dynamic ones whose essence is lost in the telling—imagine a text that dissected all the variables in the pollution problem and strung them out across myriad pages. Students are asked to remember each factor as they move on to read about the next one, and then relate earlier ones to later ones. It is easier and more effective to do this in the context of a single role and a concrete setting, gradually integrating the factors during play and in the discussion at the game's conclusion.

Take the Reconstruction period in American history, which is pivotal to an understanding of past and present problems. It is a complex and confusing period, usually presented in a dry fashion. Typically, the Reconstruction is described in terms of the various congressional plans for dealing with the South after the Civil War, a few key events — such as the impeachment of President Andrew Johnson, the shifting composition of political parties and, to some extent, the quality of life and politics for various groups in the South. Rarely, however, does the wealth of detailed data convey a comprehensible picture of the essential elements: the fate of millions of former slaves, without economic or political power, living amidst their former masters; the conflict in American political ideology that made it impossible to gain support for redistributing the wealth, or land, of the South to insure freedom to former slaves because that would have violated the fundamental belief in the right to own property; the inertia and bulk of a political system composed of divergent interests that could not agree on a resolution of the conflict. It is a fascinating and frightening drama, containing the seeds of the present American dilemma and some of the tools for its alleviation.

In a game about the Reconstruction, students assume the roles of various southern actors (freedmen, farmers, plantation owners); the shifting congressional stance is externally introduced by changes in the game rules rather than through individual players. Not all of the details of people, bills, and events can be presented in the game, of course. But the essential relationships of the major groups in the South to each other, to the rest of the country, and to the laws of the land as represented in and by Congress, can be grasped as the game proceeds. Few assert or insist that students remember the details presented in text; probably more is learned and remembered from a game that does not present the fine detail but focuses instead on the basic dilemma.

So many of the issues, processes, and problems taught in school are highly complex. And partly by virtue of that fact, they suffer the equally unfortunate fates of presentation through overwhelming detail or of simplification to the point of insignificance and dullness. Games obviously cannot and should not be used for all instruction; but they can play a key role in synthesizing a vital and complex issue. By providing insight into one major problem or facet of a problem, games can facilitate study of the details of a larger problem. The game described above aids in a specific study of the Reconstruction period, and synthesizes previous learning about the Civil War. Thus it serves as a central vehicle for a broad area of investigation.

During a semester, the social studies teacher can select four or five issues that are complex, significant, and central to the course of study. A game on each will help to provide handles on the broader topics of the course, and serve as a pivot for synthesizing themes and problems that might be lost in a myriad of detail.

Since students find many subjects dull or complex, teachers may well ask how frequently games should be used. One simple answer is that games should be used only for issues of primary importance, difficult as it may be to admit that not everything that is taught is crucial. Because games often synthesize several issues, one major topic is probably appropriate. Too much of anything is boring, and an entire curriculum of games would only saturate students. Once a month, or approximately a quarter of the curriculum, is probably the optimum allocation. The games might function to introduce a topic, motivate students, and acquaint them with the broad outlines of the problem at hand. A game could also be a culminating activity, synthesizing the study of an issue. Fortunately, no formula exists for the frequency and application of games — the choice is ultimately the teacher's.

Games for Problem Solving and Decision Making

Rarely does the development of problem-solving or decision-making ability appear on a list of course objectives. Nevertheless, these skills are implicit objectives that have become more explicit in recent years. No courses are devoted to cultivating these skills, and they transcend specific subjects. Such abilities, by their nature, are transferable from one set and type of problems to another.

If educators wish to develop problem-solving and decision-making abilities in their students, games provide an excellent vehicle. As noted earlier, most games emphasize the non-factual, process-oriented, problem-solving approach. The subject matter of a game is not particularly important if the broader objective is that of cultivating decision-making skills. A teacher need only select a game that fits his curriculum and also requires decision making by the players. By examining a game, the teacher can easily discover how much it depends on chance or on relatively mechanical operations, and the opportunities it offers for player initiative and action. Even highly programmed games — ones that are tightly constructed to limit the possible outcomes, or that are weighted to give some players greater flexibility — provide ample opportunities for player action. The players in these programmed situations usually do not know that their options are structured to result in one of a very few game solutions; they must still exercise initiative and make decisions while playing.

Games for Practice

Interpersonal relations and situations requiring experience comprise another area, usually peripheral in the curriculum, where games are more effective than conventional material. Many schools try to teach students how to behave at a job interview, for instance. This is a perfect subject for gaming; students can play themselves as well as the interviewers, and evaluate their own effectiveness. No amount of reading or drilling about behavior and decorum at an interview can substitute for practice in a real or make-believe situation.

There are other school situations where practice or experience is more valuable than reading, lectures, or lists of guidelines. In counseling, a student is usually offered much written information on possible careers and the qualifications required. Games could be used as an additional aid to give a student experience with the opportunities, decisions, and limitations he would face in a particular career. Few students select a career in high school or even early in college. But early acquaintance with the nature of—not simply the requirements for—a specific occupation can aid the student in realistically assessing his interests and capabilities.

Games and the Class Profile

The composition of the class is a key factor in deciding to use a game. Whether the class consists of students of diverse ability levels, slow learners, or gifted students will influence the decision. When and how often a game is a more effective choice than other media varies with the kind of students involved.

Diverse Ability Levels. Many teachers confront the problem of having students so widely disparate in experience and ability that the class must be subdivided into ability groups. This practice is basically undesirable. It divides the teacher's attention and complicates the problem of supervision. Students engaged in one activity distract other students quietly reading by themselves. It creates social divisions in the classroom and limits interaction among students.

Games can perform valuable functions in this type of class. In the first place, they allow students to interact on an equal footing. The problem of the chosen few can be eliminated. There is no guarantee that students of higher ability will necessarily win the game. Games lend an egalitarian atmosphere to the class, and provide equal opportunity for all to learn.

The use of educational games in a mixed class also relieves the teacher of having to circulate to make sure everybody is occupied while he tries to conduct an activity with one particular group. And, of course, teachers are human. Most would prefer to work with children who respond well and learn fast. In a game there is no reason for anyone to be neglected.

Also beneficial is the chance for students who are otherwise separated from each other to interact. Often, students of low achievement level do not wish to work with students of high achievement. In a game situation, especially where there are teams, students of both levels should be mixed so that they must work together. The experience of doing so has social as well as educational value. Students learn from each other, the less able imitating and learning from the more gifted. This phenomenon is receiving increasing attention and school systems are experimenting with having older children teach younger ones. Apparently, both learn from the experience.

An interesting question arises in this context. Imitating other students in conventional classroom activities commonly goes under the name of cheating. In games, students who do not quite see what to do will observe their classmates and imitate, step by step, the actions they take. Eventually, they learn the procedure and make their own decisions. But the practice runs counter to the fundamental classroom tenet of doing one's own work. If there is a choice between students learning from each other by imitation or not learning at all, the classroom rule can be suspended at least for the duration of the game.

Slow Learners. Games offer the most promising benefits for slow learners. Many of these children have had unpleasant experiences in classroom situations. They tend to be withdrawn or apathetic. They have short attention spans. Generally, they receive little reward for little achievement. Their relationship to the teacher, and most likely to all adult authority figures, has been unsatisfactory. Often, their facility with written materials is poor, and motivation is definitely a problem. For these students, games can literally work wonders. It is a medium they understand and participate in outside of school. They interact with peers in a situation where the teacher is either a participant or a referee, not a threat. Emotional problems will not be solved by games, but emotions that would otherwise interfere with learning can be vented in some active role playing. Reading material can be limited in a game situation and it can be made critical to the game so that students are motivated to read it. A striking example of how slow learners can be stimulated occurred in a tryout of a game, played by the designers and a group of disadvantaged teen-age boys. Some of the boys were functionally illiterate. Players were racketeers and policemen competing for the loyalty of the city block teams. In certain instances, communication was limited to written notes. When one of the block leaders was captured by the racketeers, the two boys who were left, though almost illiterate, managed to write a note to their imprisoned partner.

For slow learners, the school system has failed. There is little to lose and much that can be gained by introducing active, exciting devices such as educational games. Time and again, game designers and teachers have been surprised by the performance of participants in a game. The brightest, as measured in the usual classroom activities, do not necessarily win the game or develop particularly clever strategies. For slow learners, this is an especially pertinent point. They are not condemned to finish last. Games frequently demand and reward abilities in problem solving and decision making; very often, slower students are more adept in these activities than their more literate classmates. Perhaps the strongest argument for using games with slow learners is that the activity offers them a rare opportunity for experiencing success in the classroom.

Gifted Children. Every teacher's joy is a classroom of gifted children. Anything works with bright, motivated children. They learn from, and sometimes in spite of, the materials available. Success in school is partly a matter of figuring out the system and these children are particularly sensitive to cues and signals that suggest the right things to do and say. Sometimes the bright children get out of school knowing very little because they have jumped through the required number of hoops; they have been motivated to do the requisite things to get good grades. As a result, they are often completely receptive to everything they are taught and question little. They may learn but they don't necessarily think.

For this reason, games are valuable with a group otherwise free of classroom problems. The bright students have beaten those features of the system that operate as a threat for slow learners—teachers and grades, particularly. In a game, none of these features operate. The player must develop a strategy for achieving his objectives in the game. He must analyze and synthesize, comprehend and evaluate. He cannot get away with just memorizing.

More significantly, games can stimulate the gifted student to go beyond the few givens. Not only can games be made more complex if the class can handle easier versions, but they do not have an easily identifiable ceiling on what can be learned. Even after a student has mastered the rules and developed a winning strategy, he will have to respond to new circumstances if the game is played again. He can learn the basic facts presented in a game, but it will be a while before he has exhausted the possible relationships between them.

One student in an affluent and excellent school played the game of Market, described in Chapter 1. When the game was over, she exclaimed, "My goodness, it's the theory of supply and demand!" Undoubtedly she had understood the theory earlier, but the distinct impression remained that, until she had played the game, she had learned more about the labels than the process.

CHAPTER 3

GAMES CHILDREN PLAY

3

Elementary School Games

Junior and Senior High School Games

Computer Games

It is currently more fashionable to talk about the game technique than to use it. As with most new things, the problem is a matter of dissemination, a process requiring several steps. The originator develops his wares and, convinced of their utility, sets out in search of a buyer. In the case of educational materials, this will probably be a foundation or organization dedicated to furthering progress in education, or an affluent school system with resources of its own or access to government aid. With some luck, it isn't long before a few schools are experimenting with the new material and, if it's any good, a great many others are talking about it. But the talk certainly exceeds the use until the key link is made.

When the talk becomes loud enough, the least reputable institution in the educational world, the manufacturer or the publisher, gets involved. Whatever good he may wish to accomplish, the man who makes money is suspect. But he is critical, indispensable to progress as the mediator between the innovator and the public. Without him, the developers sit isolated in their think tanks, a few children derive advantage from the innovations, and a great many people talk about it all until they get tired of talking and forget about it.

Typical or not, this represents a brief developmental history of educational games. University groups, nonprofit (as well as profit-making) organizations, and a few school systems are experimenting with educational games. Fortunately, the final stage of regretful oblivion has not been reached. Nor does it threaten to be. Publishers and manufacturers are interested in educational games and have made initial efforts at distributing them. At present, a few educational games can be purchased commercially; more will be available soon.

For the teacher who wishes to use educational games now, this situation is not entirely satisfactory, particularly because the games on the market may be neither in his subject area nor at his grade level. Or they may be computer games for which he does not have the equipment. (Many available games can be adapted for different grade levels, though; how to do this is discussed in Chapter 5.)

The following game descriptions are presented as an aid for the teacher who wishes to survey current and potential offerings. Even if these particualr games do not suit the reader's purposes, the collection should serve to indicate the range of games likely to be available in the near future — or at least the range of subjects to which games may be applied. An exhaustive catalog is not intended here, and the inclusion or omission of specific games is not a judgment of their quality. Some experimental games for which no marketing plans now exist are included to suggest the wide variety of possible applications. (See page 196 for a chart summarizing the subject areas, grade levels, and availability of the games described.)

Elementary School Games

Get Set: Reading-Readiness Games

Games available from Houghton Mifflin Company.

This is a set of eight games for teaching basic consonantal reading methods. They are for teams of one to four players between the ages of three and six. The series is used in co-ordination with the Harrison and McKee consonantal reading system. The first games are reading-readiness games to develop sounds differentiation and context understanding. The others facilitate beginning reading and the consonantal groupings used by Harrison and McKee. Illustrations are used in the easier games; a combination of illustrations and letters are used in the others. The games are:

1. Silly Sentences — context; illustrations only
2. Stopdots — punctuation and phrasing; illustrations only
3. Animal Race — beginning sounds; illustrations and letters
4. Broken Letters — beginning sounds; illustrations and letters
5. Dominoes — letter-sound associations; illustrations and letters
6. Pickafit — context, letter-sound associations; illustrations and letters
7. Picture Words — context, reading; illustrations and words
8. Word Train — reading; illustrations and words

Detailed descriptions for five of the games follow.

Silly Sentences. The game teaches the children to discriminate among spoken meanings. The teacher tells a "silly story" stressing the "silly words." An example is, "A big lion came into the desk and ate all the walls. He was so shiny he never had enough to think, so airplanes kept away from him." The team members discuss the story and decide what sensible words they think should replace the "silly" words. They then state aloud their new version of the story. Teams may challenge other team's stories, and conflicts are resolved by vote. The game is won by the team making the greatest number of sensible word substitutes in a fixed time.

Stopdots. The game focuses on understanding the period and the comma. It also uses the left-to-right principle, and gives players a sense of the shape of a simple sentence. Large and small squares are used to simulate words; the squares are interspersed with periods and commas. Each child has a set of colored squares. For each square on the board, he places one of his own squares of the same size. Play continues until he cannot lay down a square of the appropriate size or until he arrives at a period. When a period is reached, the child says "period" and stops, and lets the next player have his turn. When a comma is reached, the child must say "comma" and then change to a lighter color; he continues to use that color until a stop is indicated. If a child fails to pause for a comma or stop for a period, all the squares that he has placed are taken away. The winner is the child who uses the the most squares.

Pickafit. Children learn to associate words with the right context in this game, which supplements the first unit of the McKee reader, "Using Spoken Context." The board shows four scenes: a kitchen, a street, a circus, and a farm. There are ten picture cards to match each scene; for instance, the farm cards include a cow, a fence, a horse, and a barn. Five wild cards (for example, a girl and a boy) matching more than one scene are also used. The cards are distributed among the players, who take turns making sentences with their cards; a player may make only one sentence and refer to only one scene at a time.

The sentences are evaluated by the other players to see if the sentences make sense or if the words belong in context. When the sentence is considered correct, the cards are placed on the appropriate scene. The winner is the player who uses up all his cards first.

The Pickafit cards have the pictures and words printed on one side and the printed words alone on the other side. In the advanced version of the game, only the printed side is used.

Animal Race. This game teaches the children to identify beginning sounds of words; it is keyed to the McKee reader, using the letters introduced in various units. The child is given a card that shows and labels an item — for example, a picture of a fork with the word *fork*. There is a printed board with pictures of animals, and an appropriate label next to each picture — dog, goat, fox, mouse, and so on. The object is to match a card with the right picture — that is, the picture whose label has the same initial consonant as is used on the card.

The players not only match cards, but may also trade cards with each other. Four children may play on a board. The game may be made more difficult by using the reverse side of each card, which has only a printed word and no picture.

Word Train. This game gives children practice in combining high-frequency words to make simple sentences, and in reading simple sentences. Although some of the words are shown both in pictures and in print, the children are encouraged to use the printed forms. Word Train can be used when the children have learned to read the high-frequency words and are learning to read other words.

The children play in two teams of two or three. Each team has an engine to mark its place on the board. The engines will be moved along two tracks outlined on the board. The word cards to fill the tracks are placed in front of the children. The high-frequency words appear only in print; the other words are printed on one side of a card and pictured on the other.

The first team starts by making a sentence or "word train" from any of the word cards. Each card fits into one space on the track. The second team reads the train. If the train is correctly read, and it makes sense, the first team moves its engine to the end of the sentence. If the second team does not read it correctly, the first team moves twice the length of the sentence. If the first team does not have a correct train, it may not move at all.

After a sentence is made and read, all the pictured words should be turned over to the printed side, to familiarize the children with the printed forms. Either side of a card may be used. Eventually the children may realize that it is to their advantage to use the printed side, as the sentence will be more difficult for the other team to read. (In an advanced version of the game, only the printed sides of the cards are used.)

After a sentence is finished, the words are returned to the front of the board. Thus only one sentence at a time appears on the board. Although the words can be used again, no sentence may be repeated. On its next turn, a team will start from the space marked by its engine. The winning team is the first one to reach the railroad station.

Games for a Social Studies Course

Information available from EDCOM Systems, Inc.

The following games are included in different units consti-
tuting a fourth-grade social studies curriculum. The course,
"Man: A Study in Adaptation," is interdisciplinary and multi-
media. It revolves around the study of five aspects of five
cultures: technology, family, life cycle, economics, and
politics in the Kikuyu, Benin, Zinacantecan, Aranda, and
Polar Eskimo cultures. Although all five topics are studied
for all five cultures, one facet is emphasized in each culture.
Accordingly the games were designed to highlight a particular area of each society.

Githaka. The name of this settlement-pattern game comes
from the Kikuyu word for the large estate of a clan. In playing
it, the children re-create the land-use system of the Kikuyu
tribe. Four to six players, as heads of households, build up
farm homesteads and polygamous families on a gameboard,
which is divided into two clans' estates.

Market Place. The game simulates the Kikuyu marketplace,
where food, housewares, hardware, jewelry, wood, and live-
stock are traded. Players go through several transactions
before they are able to obtain the items on the family shopping
lists. Thirty players, each a Kikuyu man or woman with goods,
tokens, and a shopping list, re-create the four-section marketplace as they barter goods.

Finding a Mate. This simulation demonstrates the complexity
of Aranda (Australian aborigine) kinship organization. Thirty
players, each holding an identity card as an Aranda man or
woman, search the traveling bands for a potential mate who
satisfies rigid social organization rules regulating kinship,
marriage, and clan membership.

The Tracking Game. In this board game, five to eleven players
move through the wastes of Central Australia searching for
food. Players learn to recognize subtle clues to the presence
of foodstuffs, and they re-create the division of labor between
the sexes.

Survival Game. The concept of adaptation is reviewed in this
card game. Each student determines his environment — desert,
polar, or tropical rain forest — and attempts to solve three
survival problems: food, clothing, and shelter. The five players
try to find materials on the three greatly different environment
boards to satisfy the basic survival needs shown on the cards
they have drawn.

Tool Game. This card game demonstrates how analysis of tools can provide information on how a society interacts with its environment. The game emphasizes form and function.

Hunting Game. Through this game students discover the animals the Eskimo hunts; what animals help satisfy what needs; the pros and cons of technological advancement; how the trading-post system operates; how a harsh environment with few materials limits possibilities.

Corn Game. Some of the vital decisions a Zinacantecan farmer must make, and how the quality of the land directly affects his earnings, are explored. Students play the Corn Game in order to earn money to buy positions in the Cargo System (in Cargo Game).

Cargo Game. The game helps students understand the relation between the Zinacantecans' social system and their ability to adapt to the environment through farming. Having explored the farming in the Corn Game, they now experience the other major reality in the life of a Zinacantecan man. This is the Cargo System, which defines the man's role in society and dictates how he may improve his position.

Politics in Benin. The West African kingdom's complex political organization is studied. Thirty players take different roles in selecting a new king from two equally eligible candidates, and in establishing routine collection of taxes for the new king.

Market

Information available from Industrial Relations Center, University of Chicago.

The game of Market develops understanding of the economic principles of supply and demand. It is a board game played by twenty to thirty elementary school students for a period lasting about two and one-half hours.

Action. Students play the roles of either consumer, store owner, or wholesaler. By bargaining over prices of goods, they explore the relation of supply, demand, and price level. The specific objective of each player is to maximize his own wealth or welfare. The consumers must buy enough goods to prepare four dinners before they may buy other goods. The store owner and the wholesaler try to sell the most goods for the most money.

The game is divided into two periods of about twenty minutes each. Each period has two parts, Strategy Session and Marketing Session. In Strategy Session I, players decide on the prices they want to pay or receive for goods they want to buy and sell in Market Session I. The consumers must also decide on menus for their four dinners. The store owners may want to plan a visit to a wholesaler to buy more goods or obtain something they don't already have. In Market Session I the consumers visit store owners and try to buy things they want. In Strategy Session II the players may want to reconsider their prices and advertise the prices on a chalkboard. In the final session, consumers visit store owners again.

Economy

Information available from Industrial Relations Center, University of Chicago.

This board game develops understanding of the circular flow of goods and services in the economy. It calls for twelve players and requires two or three hours to play.

Action. Several teams participate in the income flows of a simulated national economy. The groups are: machine-shop owners, manufacturers of consumer goods, heads of families, and bankers. The game's structure permits the student to learn how the interactions among the economic actors result in the distribution of goods and services on the one hand, and financial resources on the other. The government is introduced by means of chance cards to impress the student with the effect of federal taxation and expenditure in the allocation of resources.

The object of each of the players is to increase his wealth as much as possible. The machine-shop owners hire workers, and produce and sell machines to the manufacturers of consumer goods. The manufacturers of consumer goods hire workers, and produce and sell consumer goods to the families. The bankers make loans to players and collect interest payments. The family men take jobs with the manufacturers and the machine-shop owners; they pay for consumer goods, taxes, and rent, and they put savings in the bank. The winners are the wealthiest players in each category.

Kolkhoz

Information available from Board of Cooperative Educational Services.

Kolkhoz teaches the economic philosophies upon which the collective farm runs, general principles of economics as they

apply to the collective farm operation, and some of the practical details of running a collective farm. It is a board game to
be played by six junior high school students and requires
two hours.

Action. Four of the players represent farmers, one represents
the farm's manager, and the last represents the government's
GOSPLAN (planning department). The goal of the farmers is to
make the most money for the least amount of work. The
manager's goal is to satisfy government production requirements and to surpass that minimum if possible. The goal of
the GOSPLAN representative is to get the most production
at the least cost to the state.

The players interact in cycles, each of which represents a
year. The farmers must allocate their time between private
plots and the collective farm. The manager supervises the
farm's activities, tries to influence the quota, and encourages
the farmers to work. The GOSPLAN representative checks on
the manager, sets the quota, and aids the manager with
problems.

Sierra Leone

Information available from Board of Cooperative Educational
Services.

Problems and economic conditions of newly independent
African countries are explored; specific facts about the geography and recent history of Sierra Leone are also presented.
The game exists in manual and computer form. The manual
version can be played by one to four players; the computer
version is played by one student at the sixth grade level.

Action. The pupil plays the part of an A.I.D. officer in modern
Sierra Leone. Before the game starts, he is given a simulated
tour of the country and must pass a short examination on its
geography before proceeding further. He is then assigned, in
turn, to each of the three provinces of Sierra Leone where he
must give advice to the local administrators about their economic problems — land reclamation, price control, and, possibly, gross national product allocations. If he is successful
in advising the country on these problems, he is promoted
within A.I.D. and finally rotated back to Washington.

Seal Hunting

Information available from Educational Development Center.

The game dramatizes the importance of seal hunting in the
Netsilik culture, and illustrates the relation of the seal to

Eskimo mythology and kinship. It demonstrates the essentially chance interaction of the seal and Eskimo worlds, shows the psychological and economic advantages of cooperative hunting, and gives an accurate simulation of the strategy and skill involved in the winter seal hunt. Seal Hunting requires eight players and lasts two hours.

Action. Four players act as Eskimo hunters and attempt to . catch as many seals as possible during the day-long expedition represented by one play of the game. Four other players represent eight seals attempting to catch every fish; doing so allows them to return to safety at the bottom of the sea. The game uses a vertical gameboard, which prevents the two teams from viewing one another's actions. This simulates the chance interaction of the two independent worlds of the seal and Eskimo.

The seals begin the action by leaving the center of the board, which represents the bottom of the sea. They pursue fish or go to hunting holes, as directed by a spinner. The Eskimos leave camp as a group, arrange themselves at hunting holes, and try to harpoon seals that come up to breathe. If a seal is harpooned, all the hunters participate in the ritual blood drinking. Then the successful hunter goes to a new hole and the others return to their original holes. Play continues until the hunters decide they have enough meat or until time is called.

Bushman Exploring and Gathering

Information available from Educational Development Center.

This two-phase game teaches fifth-grade students the concept of cultural adaptation—the ways in which man deals with his physical environment. The game demonstrates subsistence economy in a harsh environment, the Kalahari Desert of Southwest Africa. Skills developed in the game include the use of coordinates, basic arithmetic, symbol systems, social cooperation, and role playing. Bushman is a board game for four to eight players, and requires one hour for each of the two phases.

Action. In phase one, Exploring, players represent explorer groups constructing their own map of an uncharted area. Explorers travel about the board within the limitations of their water supply. Each new square on the board is described by the appropriate card in a manual data bank. Players pick out relevant information and record it on the map grid, using a symbol system of their own invention.

In phase two, Gathering, which can take place on the second day of play, players take on new roles as heads of small bushman families. Players must locate the scarce food supplies. They are limited by chance weather cards, and by the relation between their family size and the water supply.

Caribou

Information available from Educational Development Center.

Designed for a social science course in elementary schools, the game simulates an Eskimo hunt for caribou. Two to ten players participate, and five hour-long sessions are needed.

Action. The game is played around a large board representing a 120-square-mile area of Canada's Simpson Peninsula. Hills, camp sites, caribou paths, ice-hunting lakes, and other features are shown. There are two kinds of players — the family of Eskimo hunters, and a player who represents the forces of nature. Using a program, this player varies the location and direction of the herd, wind direction, and other chance happenings in nature. A set of rules governs the detection and hunting of the caribou. One such rule reads: "From the top of a hill an Eskimo can see a herd of caribou at a distance of four miles; but when not on a hill, this distance is cut in half."

Three kinds of hunt are simulated in different sessions. One is the *taalun* hunt, where a funnel-like stone structure is used to trap the caribou. Mythology and history are introduced here, for there is a myth about this type of hunt. The children thus learn about Netsilik cosmology and social organization in playing the game.

Pollution

Information available from Wellesley Schools Curriculum Center.

The game teaches the economic and technological causes of pollution and the political, economic, and technological requirements for abating it. The game is for twelve to sixteen players at the fourth to sixth grade levels.

Action. The players are given profiles describing citizens of a small New England town. In the first phase, the players learn that as they produce goods, they also pollute the air and the water. The effects of pollution become more and more evident as the game proceeds. In the second phase, when the problem is acute, the players assemble for a town meeting to negotiate on measures for the control of pollution. The players must reach a unanimous decision about the means of control, and how it should be financed. Short- and long-term consequences of not controlling pollution are played out and individual citizens suffer. They may then renegotiate to make further efforts.

Junior and Senior High School Games

Colony®

Game available, as part of a set, from Science Research Associates, Inc.

Colony® is one of six games developed as part of a junior high school curriculum in American history. The topic and objectives of each game were selected to highlight major issues and processes, in keeping with the overall philosophy of the course. The six-game set was designed in conjunction with an American history textbook.

Colony® illustrates the basic relation that existed between the American colonies and Great Britain in the eighteenth century. Although the game is not tied to specific events and dates, it is set in the period after the French and Indian War when Britain faced a huge war debt plus increased costs of administering and defending its colonies.

The game poses the problem of the British government's need for increased revenue and its difficulty in obtaining it from available channels, that is, from taxes on trade. For colonists unaccustomed to enforcement of trade regulations, British efforts to collect revenue were irritating and appeared to be a new policy violating colonial liberty. Actually, Britain imposed stricter revenue policies throughout the empire; the colonies were not singled out for economic exploitation.

Although the game focuses on the economic conflict between Britain and the colonies, it does not expound an economic interpretation of the causes of the American Revolution. Rather, the game demonstrates that Americans did not suffer economic hardship from enforcement of trade regulations. It shows that though the arena of conflict was economic, the basic issue in contention was who should rule America. Although political elements of the conflict are not included in the game, recommendations for tying economic and political issues in postgame discussion are included for the teacher.

Players. The game is designed for an entire class. Four or five students play the British government team. Four students function as bankers for various trade centers. The rest of the students play colonial merchants, who have home bases in the southern, middle, or northern colonies.

Game Materials. A number of gameboards are the foci for game action. These include boards representing the American coastline, the interior of the continent, West Indian and European trade banks, British trade banks, and a British tax chart. In addition, play money, trade forms, and a variety of cards are utilized.

Action. The boards are placed in various parts of the room to avoid crowding. The bankers and the British government team are stationed at their respective boards; colonial merchants circulate to perform activities at each.

The objective of the merchants is to make as much money as possible. The objective of the British government team is to collect a fixed amount of money by the end of the game to pay the cost of governing the colonies. In effect, these two opposing teams play according to different rules. To achieve their objectives, the British may set taxes on various commodities traded in the game. To enforce collection, they may allocate administrative resources such as warships, customs officials, judges, and troops. But activating any of these resources costs the British money, representing salaries and maintenance costs. Thus to obtain money, they must expend some. The British, however, must avoid spending so much on enforcement that they gain little or nothing in collection. Historically, the British actually spent four times as much on enforcement as they collected from taxes on trade.

To achieve their objectives, the colonial merchants buy manufactured goods in Britain and sell them at a profit in North America. They export raw materials from the colonies and sell them to Great Britain. Purchase and sale of goods is conducted with bankers at the various locales. Prices of goods are marked on the gameboards and players keep track of their decisions on trade forms. Merchants may also buy and sell goods in foreign ports where profits may be higher but risks of getting caught in illegal trade are greater.

The choreography of the game consists of players purchasing goods in America, then moving on to the foreign trade posts at other sections of the classroom to sell these goods and purchase others. Upon returning to America to sell imported goods, they also have the opportunity to invest in colonial industry, which was for the most part illegal. Each investment, recorded by means of a Deed Card, brings the player a fixed income every round.

A major confrontation in the game occurs when players return to the American-coastline board after trading overseas. Here they face the decision of whether to pay the taxes established by the British government team or to smuggle the goods into the colonies. (If merchants have purchased illegal goods in foreign ports, they *must* smuggle.) The coastline board has numbered coves; merchants select a cove through which to enter, and check its number on a Smuggling Sheet. Meanwhile, the British check on their Smuggling Sheet the number of any coves at which they are stationing customs officials or warships. When the two Smuggling Sheets are turned over, merchants learn whether they have been caught. The British must pay for all warships and customs officials deployed, whether or not they have caught smugglers. A smuggler caught by a warship loses half the value of his cargo. A smuggler caught by a customs official, however, still has an opportunity to get off free.

The merchant may choose to intimidate the customs official by calling for popular support. For this, he draws a Mob Card. Should he lose this showdown, he may attempt to bribe an official by laying down money on the board and choosing a Bribe Card. This tells him whether the official accepts the bribe, is honest, or is greedy. In the latter two situations, he must go to court. Again, he has a chance to get off free. He may be acquitted by a colonial jury (a frequent historical occurrence), fined lightly, or tried by a judge of the Admiralty Court, who may order him to pay a stiff fine. Since the British team has Judge Cards, they may pay to add judges to the Court deck in order to increase the chances of conviction of smugglers.

At this point, the merchants have done one of the following:
1. traded legally and paid the duty
2. smuggled and got away with it
3. smuggled and got caught by a warship, and then were fined heavily
4. smuggled and got caught by a customs official who
   a. was rendered ineffective by the mob
   b. was bribed
   c. succeeded in getting the smuggler to court where he was
      (1) acquitted by a jury
      (2) fined by a jury
      (3) fined heavily by a judge

Other details of the conflict appear in the investment decisions of the merchants. Colonial industry was largely forbidden in the classic mercantile relationship because it reduced the market for manufactured goods from the mother country. In the game this is particularly evident in the case of iron. The price of iron in Britain is actually higher than what it can be sold for in America. From the merchant's point of view, it is therefore foolish to import iron, and the British iron industry suffers accordingly. In reality, the British passed a law forbidding the building of new iron foundries but it was ignored.

The fur trade also aggravates the conflict between Britain and the colonies. Unlike other commodities in the game, the price of fur is not fixed. Merchants select a chance card to find the price they must pay. Occasionally, they find that an Indian war is on, requiring British involvement in the form of troops to protect the colonies. The expenses of defending the colonies are thus weighted against the British.

As the game progresses, industry is built up in North America, more land is settled, trade expands, and the wealth of the colonies increases. So does the British effort to reap some benefit from the increase. But the British are doomed to fail. The old system of taxing trade for the purpose of regulating its direction proved an inadequate source of revenue. Fundamental alterations in the imperial relationship were required by British statesmen, and political theory was inadequate to meet the challenge.

Nevertheless, the British government team may win in the game. The chances are heavily stacked against them (although this is not immediately obvious to players) but it is not impossible for the British to collect the required amount of money. The colonial merchant with the most money at the end of the game wins among the merchants.

The game attempts to present a balanced picture of the British and colonial viewpoints. The British are not "tyrants" who try to milk the colonies of their wealth. The colonists are not suffering defenders of liberty, fighting oppression. Both have valid objectives and attitudes. Students thus learn not only the detailed operation of mercantile trade relations, but are given a basis for evaluating typical, simplified economic interpretations of the causes of the Revolution.

Frontier®

Game available from Science Research Associates, Inc.

Some of the reasons for the economic, political, and social differences that evolved in the Northwest and Southwest sections of the United States are illustrated in Frontier.® The game is intended to enrich the study of American westward expansion by focusing on process rather than the more usual account of the acquisition of particular territories. It also emphasizes fundamental sectional differences that are important to an understanding of the Civil War.

The preexisting beliefs of settlers in the two sections represented an important reason for differential development; however, this element is not explicitly represented in the game.
For example, the Northwest Territory was settled by New En-
glanders who brought with them commitment to education
and habits of town government and community action. This
was reinforced by the Northwest Ordinance, which established
the guidelines for settlement, and by economic considerations
that made community cooperation a critical factor in individual
success. While the game emphasizes economic and geographic
influences on patterns of settlement, it is not the intention to
suggest that economic considerations predetermined the differences between the two sections.

Essentially, the designers did a cost-benefit analysis of the
settlement decisions operating in the two sections. Transportation to the East, for example, was important to the prosperity
of Northwestern farmers. The enormous cost of building canals
could not be borne by a few individuals. Cooperation in the
form of investment and community taxes was required to
expand transportation facilities, and cheaper transportation
benefited everyone. The Southwest, in contrast, had an extensive network of natural waterways. Investment in transportation was thus of marginal benefit to an individual. The purchase
of more slaves or more land was much more profitable for
cultivators of cotton. For wheat farmers in the Northwest,
where labor and cash were limited, the purchase of more land
was not particularly profitable in the early phases of settlement. Thus decisions influenced by these considerations result in small farms in the Northwest, a relatively egalitarian
political structure, and community action and cooperation.
In the Southwest—where settlers began with slaves and more
money than Northwesterners—large holdings, little investment in public improvements, and a hierarchical political
structure prevail.

Players. The game is designed for an entire class. Half the class
plays in the Northwest, half in the Southwest. Each half of the
class is divided into small groups of three or four students
representing families. Two students also function as bankers,
one in each section.

Game Materials. Several gameboards are used. One represents farmland in the Northwest; another, farmland in the
Southwest. Each team also receives a Crop Profit Chart indicating prices received for grain or cotton, adjusted for the
type of transportation used to get the crop to market. In addition, each uses a Town Meeting Chart that indicates the cost of

additional land plots and the cost of public improvements (levied per land plot) depending upon the total number of plots settled. Other materials are: play money, cards representing improvements paid for, cards representing luxury items such as carriages and furniture (available only in the South), and chips representing family laborers and slaves. A set of Farmers' Almanac Cards are also included; these indicate changing conditions of credit, minimum number of plots which may be purchased, land prices, and the basic price of grain and cotton in a particular year (adjustments for transportation indicated on Crop Profit Chart).

Action. Players sit around the land board representing their section. Northwest and Southwest teams play independently of each other. The objective of each family is to increase its wealth. This is measured in terms of cash, land value (which increases with community improvements), slaves, and appropriate luxury goods.

Families start with different cash resources. In the Southwest, the variance is great to emphasize the importance of cash and slaves. (Some families start with $8000 and five slaves; one begins with $160 and one slave; one with $169 and no slaves).

The basic action of the game consists of purchasing land, borrowing money, allocating labor to cultivate the land, collecting profits and paying debts, and meeting to consider community projects. A Farmers' Almanac Card is turned over at the beginning of play, and the information it contains (land price, credit, minimum acreage for purchase, and so on) is circled on the Crop Profit and Town Meeting Charts. Each family in turn then proceeds to purchase land by paying the price to the team's banker and fencing in the plots with a marker on the gameboard.

The game is structured so that in the Northwest every family can afford the down payment on the minimum amount of land (four plots). In subsequent rounds, each family must make its annual payment to the bank for land (and in the Southwest, for slaves) purchased on credit.

The prices of land, minimum acreage requirements, and credit rules simulate real conditions in the period between 1815 and 1830. The actual prices are not used, but the pattern is accurate: The fluctuations, the eventual reduction of the minimum purchasable acreage, and the removal of credit all reflect responses to an economy expanding so rapidly on shaky credit that it suffered severe panics periodically.

Once players have purchased land, they cultivate it by placing a labor chip on one plot. Slavery is forbidden in the

Northwest, and cotton can be cultivated only with slaves. Thus Northwestern families are indirectly obliged to cultivate grain with available family labor. The rule about slavery reflects the provision in the Northwest Ordinance. In the Southwest, the family without any slaves cannot cultivate cotton. Since cotton brings a higher profit, this family is very poor compared to others in the section. The family with only one slave cultivates cotton and grain. Each family receives a profit for each land plot under cultivation *except one* that represents the subsistence or living costs of the family. The surplus is sold for profit.

When the basic economic activities are completed, each sectional team meets as a community. One player is selected as mayor to conduct the town meeting. Players then consider investing in public improvements; the choices consist of schools, a town hall, roads, and canals. In the first round of the game, neither team is likely to vote for improvements since they have little money to pay for them. The cost per family in taxes decreases as more settlers arrive; in each round, four land plots are automatically fenced in to represent the influx of new (symbolic) settlers. Thus, as the game proceeds, the cost of improvements declines. On the other hand, players are stimulated to pay for improvements to hasten this process since each improvement increases the number of new, symbolic settlers above the automatic four; thus it becomes even cheaper to invest in subsequent improvements.

The optimum strategy in the Northwest is to make all improvements by the end of the game, beginning with the least expensive. The optimum strategy in the Southwest is to invest in land and slaves. Because the game rules reflect the need to rotate the cotton crop, Southern planters can see that they should buy more land before buying more slaves so as to have land available when older plots are exhausted.

As crop prices fluctuate, or as taxes are voted, some students may be forced to sell off plots of land to maintain loan payments to the bank. During the sixth round, or year, of the game, an overall economic crash is simulated with low prices and no credit. A ruined farmer may sell out completely and hire out his labor.

By the end of the game, the Northwest will be an area of many small, basically equal farms. The Southwest will consist of two very large plantations, one smaller farm, and a poor grain farmer (unless he has sold off and hired out). Players are not aware that the game is highly programmed to produce these results by means of the controlled resources and prices built in by the designers. Scoring is based on assets at the end of the game but is corrected for discrepancies in starting resources, so any family can win.

A postgame examination of the boards graphically illustrates the different styles of life that prevailed in the two sections. Students learn how variations in size of landholdings, along with other conditions, reflected and reinforced differences in political structures.

Reconstruction®

Game available from Science Research Associates, Inc.

The game deals with the difficulty of achieving social and political reform in the South after the Civil War. Its focal point is the dilemma of the freedmen who, though free, depended on the intervention of Congress to maintain their new political rights in the face of hostility and resistance among the governing classes of the South. Without economic power to support their freedom, the situation of ex-slaves was scarcely an improvement of their previous condition.

The game does not depict particular events in the complex postwar period, nor does it attempt to include the myriad details of relationships among Southern groups or among Northern political factions. Rather, it stresses the relation between planters, freedmen, and self-sufficient farmers.

The game begins amidst the economic disruption in the South after the Civil War. Much land was ravaged; in the game this is represented on gameboards, where the cost of planting "bad" land is higher than planting untouched land, the difference representing the costs of restoration. Southern sources of capital were exhausted, so that planters and farmers in the game cannot borrow money; thus they can afford to plant only a portion of their land. Although their situation improves as the game progresses, planters are unlikely to be able to cultivate all their land again and may even have to sell some to pay taxes.

Planters faced, too, the problem of a new kind of labor force. Paying wages to ex-slaves was probably not more expensive than slavery. The main problem was that the labor force was now mobile. Migration of some Negro families to the North and West in fact created labor shortages in some areas, thus pushing wages up. Many former slaves were eager to explore the countryside or were unwilling to work for their former master; their unavailability further reduced or altered the nature of the labor supply. And since the government had promised "forty acres and a mule," many freedmen waited for the economic independence this would bring—fearing that working for their former masters would make them slaves again.

The planters responded by the attempt to reimpose slavery, in all but name, through Black Codes. These prevented bargaining for wages and permitted freedmen to be fined for vagrancy. Since the freedmen were largely penniless, a planter could pay the fine and force the freedman to work off the debt. Slavery reconstructed was the result.

The freedmen did have some protection from the federal government, particularly in the form of the Freedmen's Bureau. This agency provided subsistence and some education to freedmen. As time passed, the Bureau attempted to get freedmen to work and tried to supervise labor agreements. However, both parties distrusted the intermediary which could not, in any case, prevent a return to former practices on the plantations.

Congress, meanwhile, passed through a number of phases of reform, roughly described as lenient, stringent, and terminal. These are simulated in the game through a set of Congress Charts that alter the rules of the game at various predetermined points. In the first phase, planters retain all their political power and can, in essence, establish Black Codes. Freedmen are at their mercy. After a few rounds, a new Congress Chart operates in the game. This one represents Radical Reconstruction; it disenfranchises some large planters and enfranchises the freedmen. Under these rules, freedmen fare best. Under the last Congress Chart, planters are reenfranchised and freedmen retain the vote. Here planters can reexert their power, even if they are too few to constitute a majority, because they control the economic power in the South. Without the protection of the Freedmen's Bureau, for example, ex-slaves must work; this dependence on planters enables the latter to control the freedmen's vote. In reality, violence and intimidation and the habit of social dependence were powerful controls on any attempt to exercise political power. In the game, these are not explicitly represented and economic dependence suffices.

Players. The game is designed for an entire class, adjustable for variations in number of students. Six students play Southern planters, eight play self-sufficient farmers, and twelve play freedmen. One student plays an agent from the Freedmen's Bureau, and another is a banker for the landowners.

Game Materials. A number of gameboards of different sizes are used in Reconstruction®. Each planter receives his own small board, representing his plantation. The farmers play around a single, larger farm board. The freedmen play around a Freedmen's Bureau board. In addition, bank boards for landowners and freedmen are used for recording various transactions. Chance cards, cards indicating cotton prices, three Congress charts, cards for the Freedmen's Bureau agent, chips, and play money comprise the other materials of the game.

Action. In effect, the landowners (planters and farmers) and the freedmen are two basic teams competing to increase their wealth. Although players operate as individuals they are scored both individually and collectively.

The game consists of political and economic activities during each round. First, players assemble for a voting session, the outcome of which determines the rules governing the subsequent economic cycle. The issues are presented on the Congress Chart (which states first who may vote) and focus primarily on whether freedmen may be fined for refusing to work, whether land should be taxed to pay for freedmen's education, and whether freedmen would be permitted to rent land. Even though this is the first activity in which players participate, they readily see the discrepancy in power, made obvious by the restrictions on who may vote and the kinds of benefits accruing to different groups when the issues are voted on.

Players then transact economic business. Planters and farmers plan the allocation of their resources for cultivation. They must pay to cultivate plots of land, and must hold enough money in reserve to pay wages to laborers in the next step of the round.

While planters and farmers make their planting decisions and pay the banker for planting costs, freedmen wait for "forty acres and a mule" from the government. Each freedman controls six labor chips. He places as many chips as he can on the Freedmen's Bureau board. The Freedmen's Bureau agent tells the freedmen how many laborers the government will pay living costs for (fifty-six in the first round, for example, leaving sixteen that must be hired out). As many farmers as the government will support are eligible to remain on the board to wait for free land. The game is structured so that the government supports a fairly large number of laborers in the early round; even with farmers hiring out some of their laborers, planters face a labor shortage relative to the number of land plots they can afford to cultivate.

In the hiring session that follows, confrontation occurs between planters who need laborers and freedmen who do not need to work. If the planters have voted to permit fining laborers who refuse work, freedmen can be forced to remove chips from the Bureau board and hire them out. This serves primarily to show the freedmen the power of the planters, and to show planters that they must coerce laborers into working.

Resolution of the economic cycle follows. The cotton price is indicated on a card, and planters and farmers collect income. The Freedmen's Bureau agent reads a card announcing which labor chips have received free land. Freedmen and any farmers who hire out then pay living costs to their respective bankers.

As the game proceeds, the government supports fewer laborers until finally it supports none at all. At the same time, planters and farmers can cultivate more and more land plots, requiring more labor. Only four land plots are given away in the game; they are worth extraordinary point bonuses to the freedmen but otherwise remain dormant, that is, uncultivated, in the game. As the Congress Charts change, however, freedmen fare better. They can vote a tax on all land plots, the proceeds of which are applied to freedmen's education. They can vote a tax on cotton to pay for additional Freedmen's Bureau cards; when placed on a plantation, these require that a planter pay more than the minimum subsistence wage. Since freedmen are penalized for any labor chips that must be supported by the government, they are induced to work.

This game is highly programmed, too, through such factors as costs and prices; the effect is that the situations of different players mesh to depict how economic and political fortunes change over a length of time. Nevertheless, landowners or freedmen may win. The free land plots carry a huge bonus for the freedmen, insuring some fair chance of closing the intrinsic gap between them and the landowners. At the end of play, however, students compare the situations of freedmen and landowners; this puts a more realistic perspective on the real value of a few land plots compared to the total wealth and power of the landowning class. They learn, too, the intricate relationship between political and economic power. Less tangible elements of the social structure of the South—such as the long tradition of slavery and the attitude of white superiority —are introduced through other media, such as a text.

Promotion®

Game available from Science Research Associates, Inc.

The complex developments of industrialization and urbanization in late nineteenth century America are synthesized in Promotion.® The growth of cities, industries, a railroad network, and mechanized agriculture are usually described sequentially; the game form provides an opportunity to demonstrate the simultaneity and interaction of these developments.

The expansion of railroads, spurred by the demands of the Union army during the Civil War, in turn increased demand for iron and steel. By creating a national market, the railroads also made possible the growth of large-scale businesses in almost every industry. This attracted large numbers of workers from the countryside and from overseas; they flocked to the job centers, producing the rapid growth of cities. Such growth would have been impossible without the increased efficiency of farming — in turn made possible by technological advance in industry itself, and by railroads connecting farm and city — which freed laborers to work in industry. The game takes its name from the entrepreneurial and exploitative spirit that characterized the age. Besides demonstrating the relations between various economic sectors, Promotion® deals with the role of individual men in building the economy. Not only were large corporations built by determined men, but cities and farm settlement were actively promoted by land speculators.

Much of the growth depended on credit, which frequently broke down, resulting in severe depressions every decade. This aspect of the economy, however, is not represented in the game. Neither is the great suffering and unequal distribution of wealth that accompanied the spectacular growth. The role of the federal government, important as it was in the country's economic growth, is not included either.

Players. The game accommodates an entire class. Students form four types of teams: two each of cities, farms, railroads, and industries (iron and steel). In addition, four bankers are assigned, one to serve each type of team.

Game Materials. A number of small gameboards and one large one are utilized. Each team receives a board on which to calculate and record decisions. Thus there are city, farm, railroad, and industry boards. Each type of banker also receives a small board to record transactions specific to the activities of the teams he serves. One large nation board is placed in front of the room so that the overall growth of the economy is illustrated throughout play. In addition, chance cards, chips, and play money are used.

Action. Each pair of teams (for example, the two city teams) compete with each other for wealth. There is no competition between different types of teams; growth in one sector of the economy stimulates growth in the others.

The basic actions of the game consist of investments by individual teams and negotiation among teams. Farm teams invest in producing grain and in equipment. City teams invest in improvements, such as water systems, that attract population. Iron and steel industries invest in production and in technological improvements that increase production capacity. Railroads invest in building track.

In a round, every team negotiates with every other, with the exception of farms and industries. This interaction would certainly be realistic; however, for purposes of simplicity it was deliberately omitted. The sequence includes the following interactions:

Cities and railroads   purchase goods from industries
Cities and farms   debate routes with railroads
Farmers   negotiate with railroads (about freight rates)
Cities   pool resources with farms (to help railroads build over preferred routes)

Any team may extend credit or make other deals with any other.

Every decision of every team has some impact on another team, or sector of the economy. Railroads gain income for every unit of track they build, representing shipping business. Since track is purchased from industry teams, their income and production are assured. Since cities gain population if a railroad passes through them, they may offer railroads a percentage of their business income as an inducement to build. This income is based on the size of the city's population. Cities gain even more population when a railroad passing through them connects with the farm regions to the west. Thus cities are stimulated to cooperate with farms and with railroads for their own self-interest. Industries may expand by paying to activate machines and by converting iron-producing to steel-producing machines.

At the beginning of the game, each railroad has only a small stretch of track; cities and industries are small; unmechanized farms produce only a small surplus of grain for a local market. The railroads are central to the growth of all teams. Farmers may not mechanize, begin large-scale production, or earn the world (as opposed to local) grain price until a railroad reaches them. And although a city may build improvements, thereby increasing its population, its main source of growth is connection by railroad with eastern markets and western produce centers. Industries sell iron and steel to cities for their improvements, but their initial growth depends on the railroads' demand. The sequence of negotiations in the game is arbitrary, providing an orderly pattern for what was essentially chaotic in history.

After all deals have been made, and production costs paid to bankers, teams collect income from their respective bankers. At this time, they may also borrow money. Repaying these loans is optional; in effect, credit is cumulatively unlimited and loans are not called in (that is, an overextending economy is permitted to proceed without panics for purposes of simplicity). At this time, too, each team picks a chance card from a deck held by its respective banker. These are included to provide texture and detail. For instance, a railroad team might draw: "Digging equipment breaks down. Lose $50."

Railroads, farms, and cities record growth on the nation board. This is controlled by the requirement that they turn in, for example, chips representing track or city improvements. (City teams have a key indicating the value in population growth of improvements, railroad connection, and so on.) Farms fence in additional land plots purchased. Industries mark on their boards any additional machines they have activated, thereby increasing production capacity.

Intervention®

Game available from Science Research Associates, Inc.

The Intervention® game illustrates America's increasing involvement in foreign affairs at the turn of this century, after the Spanish-American War. Emphasis is placed on small, frequently unstable countries, particularly in the Caribbean; European affairs are not specifically included.

The game's purpose is to show the reasons for the initially reluctant but nevertheless escalating involvement of the United States in foreign affairs. Three countries are used as examples: the Philippines, Cuba, and the Dominican Republic. These were chosen to represent different starting situations, although no attempt is made to simulate a detailed course of events in each country.

The game begins with the United States in possession of Cuba and the Philippines after the victory over Spain. Although the war was fought to help Cuba win its independence, the government maintained forces in Cuba and delayed her independence. Through independent military action, the Philippines were taken during the war and, in close debate, the treaty with Spain giving them to the United States was ratified. The Philippines are in rebellion as the game starts, Cuba is a stable colony, and the Dominican Republic a stable independent country.

Conflicting interests of a number of groups in and out of government are reflected in the game. Businessmen, State Department officials, military officials, and congressmen of varying points of view are included. The primary interest of businessmen is profit; governmental policy helps to secure American business interests in a number of ways. Stability, whether achieved through total involvement (colonies) or through little involvement, produced situations of greater benefit to businessmen than any unstable situation. State Department officials primarily aim for stability and friendliness toward the United States. Military officials have a vested interest in involvement.

The game shows how haphazard decision making was at
the time, so that the independent actions of the different groups
on the scene (such as the taking of the Philippines itself) created situations requiring official government response. Players
are permitted to take independent action in the game provided
they have the resources.

Failure to take action was often as crucial as taking action.
In the game, if no action is taken in a situation of rebellion,
for example, and anti-American forces win, the resulting anti-
American government penalizes all players. Inaction is simulated if no decision is made within a limited time period during
play, and the delay often carries undesirable results.

The game does not expound a particular foreign policy.
Rather, it simulates the various courses of action available to
the government, the consequences of action, and the frequent
need, once involved, to intervene even more in the affairs of
other nations.

Players. The game is designed for an entire class, with instructions for varying the numbers of players depending on the size
of the class. Six students play businessmen; five play State
Department officials; five play Military Department officials;
nine to eleven play congressmen, divided among isolationists,
expansionists, and uncommitted. One player serves as banker.

Game Materials. The game uses several boards. Three country
boards are used, one each for the Philippines, Cuba, and the
Dominican Republic; each has space for businessmen, state
officials, and military officials to record actions they recommend and take. One half of each country board consists of a
circle with twelve wedges. Each wedge indicates: a situation;
business income if the country is in that situation; the military
costs, represented in ships; the diplomatic or administrative
costs of remaining in that situation, represented in officials;
the actions available to the American government; and the
results of each action (in code form). The circle is covered by
a circular mask exposing only one wedge at a time. Other
materials used are: profiles describing the positions of congressmen; a Congress board on which budget decisions are
recorded; a banker's board; a treasurer's board; chance cards,
chips, and play money.

Action. The country boards are placed in different parts of the
room. These are visited by businessmen, state officials, and
military officials who, as teams, record their recommendations
(or actions if they have the resources) on the board itself.
Businessmen may also invest in plantations during their visits.

Meanwhile, the congressmen, using profiles and the Congress board in another part of the room, debate budgets for the State and Military Departments.

The basic action of the game consists of establishing and implementing a foreign policy toward each of the three countries. After teams recommend actions to be taken in each country, and Congress has tentatively decided a budget for the State and Military Departments, all players meet. Based on the actions they wish to take, the State and Military Departments may request higher budgets than Congress planned to allocate. If they fail to obtain their requests, they cannot take their first chosen action and a compromise must be reached. By controlling the budget, Congress can thus control the action. A new situation is created in a country whether or not action is taken. The cycle of recommending action, deciding on a budget, taking action, and learning the consequences of decisions is then repeated.

The outcome of some actions depends partly on chance. For example, if the government makes a rebellious American colony independent, the resulting situation may be "a stable, independent country" or an "anti-American government in power." This is determined by a color-coded chance card, which indicates how many wedges on the circle to move — thus revealing which of the two situations prevails.

Some decisions are irrevocable. For example, once Congress has paid to activate ships or officials, it cannot take them completely out of the game. The most it can do is keep ships in dry dock or keep officials in Washington — less expensive measures than keeping ships active and officials overseas. The point is that even with some retrenchment, every involvement makes it almost impossible to return to the *status quo ante* and easier to continue at the same level of operation. If military officials have enough ships to take an action, Congress *must* pay for their active use that round.

The objective of congressmen is to get reelected. They do this by acquiring sufficient points, and these in turn accrue if they succeed in establishing policies that reflect their profiles. Thus, for every round that a country is in a stable, independent situation, isolationists gain points. If expansionists prevail, isolationists may fail to acquire the requisite one hundred points and are considered ousted from office.

Businessmen buy plantations (on the country board); in every round they earn income determined by the situation prevailing in the country. For example, if an anti-American government is in power in a country, business income declines to zero. Thus businessmen attempt to influence the government to take action that will restore a situation favorable to business interests. Businessmen activate a particular situation in the

Dominican Republic, which begins as a stable, independent country. Once four plantations are bought by Americans, the wheel must be turned to an unstable situation requiring action on the part of the government.

Most of the situations in the game are unstable. Even if players do nothing, by choice or by default, new situations are created. In general, situations created this way are worse than the earlier ones. Minor involvement, particularly if followed by inaction, tends to lead to greater involvement. The composition of Congress contributes to this pattern. The even division of isolationist and expansionist congressmen, and the objective of uncommitted congressmen to limit expenditure, should cause reluctance to intervene. To remedy the resulting situations, in turn, intervention on a larger, more expensive scale is required.

The game ends after a fixed number of rounds; or it may end sooner if all three countries reach stable situations where nothing further need be done, or where players choose to do nothing more without adverse consequences.

The game is not won by one team. The businessman with the most money wins for the business team. The State Department receives points for each country in a favorable situation each round. If the team fails to earn one hundred points, it is considered fired. The Military team receives a point for every active ship every round. If it does not get eighty points, it is considered fired. Each congressman is reelected if he accumulates one hundred points at the end of the game; points, in amounts coded to the situation of each country, are awarded to the three types of congressmen after each round.

Development®

Game available from Science Research Associates, Inc.

The game of Development® explores the relations between the major world powers and the developing nations of the world. Labeled East and West, the two major powers compete, partly through foreign aid, for the loyalty of developing countries. The latter seek to improve their standard of living by accepting foreign aid without forfeiting their political independence and freedom of action in world affairs.

Loyalty of developing nations has intangible psychological value to the major powers, as well as the material benefits of trade and military bases. At minimum, the major powers seek to insure the neutrality of such nations if they cannot win their alignment. No ideological positions are defined. Developing countries may side with either major power, based on the aid they receive or even for arbitrary unexplained reasons.

Players. The game is played by an entire class. Developing countries are represented by four teams of approximately four players each. There is a Western government team and an Eastern government team, each with three players. Western businessmen form two teams of three players each. Two bankers, each serving two countries, also play.

Game Materials. The game uses a number of boards. A developing-country board is given to each of the four teams. Each board shows diverse forms of investment available to governments and private investors. A scale, to record foreign aid given by each major power, is also included.

A bank board is given to each of the two bankers.

A voting chart and a set of crisis cards are placed at the front of the room. Play money is used and different colored chips, representing foreign aid, are given to each of the major power teams.

Action. The objective of each developing country is to increase its wealth. This is measured in terms of cash from foreign aid, wages from industries built in the country, and taxes levied on industries by the country. The major powers' objective is to secure the loyalty of the developing countries; this is measured in terms of the number of votes received by each power in crisis situations. Western business teams have the objective of competing for the most wealth.

The basic action of the game consists of an aid-and-investment phase and an international-crisis phase. In the first, the major-power teams give foreign aid to the developing countries. Businessmen visit the countries and invest in industries; a portion of the resulting income goes to the country as wages paid to native workers. In the international-crisis phase, a crisis card is read. The developing countries vote either with one major power or the other on the crisis, or they remain neutral. Choosing sides can be costly. For example, if voting with one major power involves cutting off trade with a third country (not represented in the game), the developing country may have to pay out a sum of money, representing loss of trade revenue.

Developing countries may tax the foreign business investment if they wish. This brings additional income; however, it may also discourage further investment. Thus the wisest strategy for the developing country is to tax late in the game, when much industry has been built and further investment is of marginal value.

Major powers each receive twenty foreign-aid chips per round. They are restricted in the maximum number of chips they may give to a single country in any one round. This rule was made to avoid immediate polarization of two developing countries around each major power. The developing countries, too, may lose freedom of action if they accept too much aid from either major power. In any round, if a country has five more foreign-aid chips from one major power than from the other, it must vote with the former. The teams are thus encouraged to obtain all they can from both major powers without landing in either camp.

For the developing countries, the best strategy is to vote neutral (abstain) or to alternate votes each round. If major powers are unsure of the loyalty of a developing country, they are likely to continue to give it maximum aid. If, however, a developing country consistently votes for one side, the opposing major power may decide to withdraw aid and try to gain another country's loyalty instead. The business teams may be prohibited from investing in a country by the Western government team.

Pursuit

Game available from Educational Services, Reader's Digest, Inc.

The game explores developments in the civil rights movement since the mid-1950s. It illustrates the influences exerted by individual initiative, group effort, geographic location, and government action.

Pursuit examines equality of opportunity, as it existed for black Americans in recent years, in five categories: education, jobs, housing, voting, and public accommodations. The northern, middle, and southern regions of the United States are compared in the study.

Players. Three to six students may play. Players are randomly assigned to each of the three regions of the country. The objective of each is to achieve the highest possible goals in the five areas indicated above. Each player circles his goal before play begins. For example, in education a player may opt for admission to graduate school with a full scholarship, the highest goal, or settle for the opportunity to complete the sixth grade, the lowest goal. Although the obvious is to select the highest goal, it is unlikely that a player could achieve the highest goal in the period the game spans (1954–1968).

Action. The game is played on a map board, which has tracks within each region. Each circle on the tracks represents one or more of the categories in which players are attempting to achieve goals. When a player lands on a particular circle, determined by the throw of a die, he may choose to try for his goal. Thus, if a southern player lands on an education circle in 1954 and has selected a very low goal, he may try to achieve it. This is done by referring to a wheel, which calculates the education situation for that player based on the year, region, and category. The wheel directs the player to one of a set of outcome cards. The player records whatever he has achieved, as described in the outcome card, whether higher or lower than his goal. The game does reward accuracy; a player who realistically assesses his situation, and tries for and wins his goal exactly, receives bonus points.

The time period of the game advances automatically after every two rounds of play. The legal calendar describes the situation in each of the five categories, indicating new legislation as it occurs. However, the advancement of the legal calendar may be hastened by the cooperative action of two or more players. If two players land on the same topical circle (in the same of different regions) they may give up a turn in order to advance the calendar.

A player may wish to postpone trying for his goal because he believes conditions are not yet favorable; he may pass, but he loses one point. If he lands on a "wild" circle, he may try for a goal in a category he has not yet attempted. He may also use a wild circle as an opportunity to change a goal, higher or lower. (Goal-change circles also appear.) A few intersection circles exist, permitting a player who lands exactly on one to move to another region where his chances for advancement will be greater.

Players may also cooperate by demonstrating. When one player lands on a demonstration circle, he may solicit the participation of other players. The results of a demonstration are discovered through chance cards; players who have joined will gain or lose the indicated number of points on the card. The success of a demonstration itself frequently depends upon the number of players who participated in it.

The game ends after two rounds of play are completed under the 1968 legal calendar. The player with the highest number of points wins. This total includes the score or goal (whichever is lower) he achieved in each topic, with bonuses for accuracy, plus or minus points gained or lost in demonstration, or through other chance elements appearing in marked circles.

Mathematics Games

Information available from D. C. Heath & Company.

The math games described below provide an enjoyable way for students to review and practice basic arithmetic operations,

and are highly motivating by design. Four basic games, each
with variations, were devised around each of three familiar
devices: cards, dominoes, and spinners. The object of each
game is specified, such as reaching a numerical target. The
arithmetic operations required to achieve the object of the
game are, for the student, simply means to an end. Thus, by
competitive interaction in the context of games, students receive drill painlessly.

Card Games

The card games focus on addition and subtraction. The games
utilize a special deck of 105 cards, each with a numeral from
0 to 9, and several wild cards that can represent any numeral
from 0 to 9.

On the Button. Two or three players each start with two cards.
The rest of the deck remains face down. The object of the game
is to hit the target number 20 exactly, or "on the button." Each
player in turn discards a card, and adds it aloud to the total
already played. A new card from the deck is then drawn. The
player who reaches the target of 20 exactly wins the cards for
that round. When the entire deck is used up, the player with
the most cards wins the game.

If players fail to meet the target "on the button," cards that
were played remain on the table and are taken by the player
who meets the target in the next round.

If a player makes a mistake in the game, and is correctly
challenged by another player, the challenger wins all the
cards on the table at that point. If the challenge is incorrect,
the challenged player wins the cards.

Variations in the game include starting with the number 20
and using subtraction, aiming for a target number of zero.
More complicated versions of the game involve the use of
addition, subtraction, multiplication, and division in one
play.

Equation Match. Three players each receive five cards;
three cards are turned up on the board. The object of the
game is to make as many equation matches as possible. An
equation match is made when one card from the player's
hand equals the sum or difference (product, quotient) of two
cards on the board. He then makes a pile of the three cards
comprising the match. If a player cannot make a match in
his turn, he must put a card on the board. Players must
verbalize all moves; vigilant competitors may challenge
incorrect moves.

When players are out of cards in their hands, a new set

of cards is dealt and a new round begins. The player with the most matches at the end of the game (when the deck is used up) wins.

Equation Rummy. The goal of the game is to make equation rummy; this consists of four equation matches of a kind (all 2s for example) or a run of four consecutive equation matches (3,4,5,6 for example). The game operates in basically the same fashion as Equation Match.

Equals. The object of the game is to make an equation using the four cards in the player's hand. An equation can be made by finding three cards that have a sum equal to the fourth card or two pairs of cards that have the same sum. (Other arithmetic operations may be used in different versions of the game.) Each equation that the player can make consti-tutes a "book." The player then draws four new cards. If a player cannot make any equation in his turn, he discards one card and draws another from the deck. When the deck is ex-hausted, the player with the most books wins the game.

Team Equals. Players have the same object as in the game of Equals: the attempt to make an equation of four cards. In this version, however, two players work together to make an equation. A player may not communicate his intended equations to his teammate. Each player must therefore con-sider the possibilities his partner might have in mind, besides what the cards in his own hand suggest.

Domino Games

This set of games focuses on factors and multiples. A special set of dominoes with printed numerals is used.

Brick Dominoes. Two to four players each receive an equal share of the dominoes. The object of the game is to win bricks, or sets of dominoes. The player with the highest num-ber of dominoes at the end of the game is the winner.

A brick represents a series of problems and solutions. In building the brick, each player puts down a domino con-taining a numeral that supplies a missing factor in the domino above. This move not only provides his solution, but sets a problem for the next player.

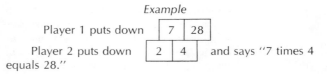

Example

Player 1 puts down   7 | 28

  Player 2 puts down   2 | 4   and says "7 times 4 equals 28."

The next player must use a domino with a 2 on it to continue play (2 × 2 = 4). Each player states his solution aloud. The last player to move on any brick wins all the dominoes in that brick. Since a player can see the other players' dominoes, he can develop a strategy to shut out his rivals and take the brick for himself.

Domino Chains. Two to four players take five dominoes each; the rest of the set remains face down.

The object of the game is to build a domino chain. The first player to build a chain wins the round; the player with the highest number of chains at the end of the game wins.

A chain consists of a set of five dominoes in which the missing factors make a consecutive run of 1 through 5 or in which the missing factor is the same. (Other chains are possible in more complicated versions of the game.)

Examples

8	8	8 × 1 = 8
3	6	3 × 2 = 6
9	27	9 × 3 = 27
7	28	7 × 4 = 28
2	10	2 × 5 = 10
4	20	4 × 5 = 20
5	25	5 × 5 = 25
2	10	2 × 5 = 10
1	5	1 × 5 = 5
3	15	3 × 5 = 15

Domino Quotients. Two to four players each take six dominoes; the rest of the set remains face down. Each player attempts to play all his dominoes. The winner of the game is the player who goes out first.

The player with the highest domino begins the game. Each player may play one domino in his turn. He must lay down, from his hand, a domino representing the quotient of the two numbers on a domino already played. It may be a domino that has the actual numeral of the quotient, *or* a domino whose quotient equals that of a previously played domino. Suppose the previously played domino has the numerals 8 and 24 (24 ÷ 8 = 3). The player could put down any domino showing the numeral 3. Or he could play a domino with, say, the numerals 2 and 6 on it (6 ÷ 2 = 3). If a player can make no move, he draws a domino from the set.

Domino Factors. This game operates in basically the same fashion as Domino Quotients. However, the domino laid down from the player's hand represents a factor (or a multiple, in one version) of a domino already played. Thus if a domino with a double 6 is on the board, a player can place next to it a domino with 1, 2, 3, or 6. The player who goes out first wins the game.

Spinner Games

The spinner games focus on fractions. A special double spinner on a card is used. Each spinner face has the numerals 1 through 10 printed on it. One face represents the numerator of a fraction, the other the denominator. The games, currently in development, emphasize practice in the following areas:
1. lowest common multiple and greatest common divisor
2. operations (addition, subtraction, multiplication, division) of fractions
3. reduction or comparison of fractions
4. mixed fractions

INS (Inter-Nation Simulation)

Game available from Science Research Associates, Inc.

The game is designed to make foreign policy and international politics understandable. Each nation has five decision makers. The time taken for a session is forty to ninety minutes and the game is designed for high school and college students.

Action. INS is an elaborate functioning construct of the major factors in the international political system. Qualitative models of each nation are created and roles are assigned to each participant. The five main roles in a nation include the head of state, a domestic opposition leader, and a foreign-policy adviser. One hundred twenty-two variables are used to describe a nation. All the main political, economic, and military variables or indications are quantified so that the resultant quantities can be added to get an index. An attempt is made to weigh the variables of a nation realistically. For example, the U.S.A. has a figure of 73 for variable 16, consumption satisfaction (percent).

The players try to achieve certain goals and strategies by means of force, bargaining, or trade. The results that their actions, and those of other nations, have on the country are then calculated by means of equations representing relationships between the variables.

INS can be described as a bold attempt at applying a systems approach to political decision making. The simulation has the advantage of being highly flexible. It can be used for any nation and any set of nations — provided the relevant information for the variables is obtainable, and assuming, for game purposes, that the relationships do not vary with time and geography.

Crisis

Game available from Simile II.

The problems that nations have in resolving their international tensions is simulated in Crisis. Teams of three to six high school students play the game, which is a simplified version of the Inter-Nation Simulation.

Action. The goals for each team are to secure a rare element called Dermatium for their country, and to prevent the destruction of their nation. Thus the teams are under pressure to act aggressively to secure the element, but are constrained by the fear of war.

The players are required to make decisions at various periods in the simulation; they may also participate in alliances, world police forces, fact-finding commissions, and summit conferences. They may send and receive messages; in addition, they have world histories to read, but different versions are given to different teams.

Grand Strategy

Game available from Games Central, Abt Associates, Inc.

This game simulates international relations and diplomacy in a wartime crisis situation. It is played by twenty to fifty high school students or adults, and requires one to two hours.

Action. Ten or more nations are represented, depending on the number of players. The players represent either the chief of state or the chief of staff. Their objective is to achieve their nation's political aim at minimum military and economic costs. The time period covers the five years from 1914 to 1918. The players are seated around a table facing a blackboard. An outline of the European continent is sketched on the blackboard. The number of army divisions and naval ships deployed is written in the appropriate locations. Each nation chooses sides, forming alliances and friendships. Then units of the army and navy are deployed in the country of origin or abroad. The referee then asks each country to state its position. The nations may change position until all positions are formalized. Engaged armies suffer attrition at the rate of 10 percent each year. If they are not engaged, the status quo remains. A war victory requires a 2 to 1 superiority. Ocean transport requires 2 to 1 dominance of transit routes by naval forces. The alliances may then change. There is a certain degree of historical accuracy but it is not necessary to have the same outcome as in 1918.

Dangerous Parallel

Game available from Scott, Foresman and Company.

How nations make policies in the face of a specific international situation is simulated. Six teams are needed to play with one to five players per team. The game is for high school students; minimum playing time is one hour although the game is intended to be used in four one-hour sessions.

Action. Each of six teams represents a country involved in a fictionalized foreign policy crisis, which is actually a disguised simulation of the Korean situation. Members of each country team have different cabinet roles. Negotiation sessions alternate with policy moves. All countries simultaneously display one of their four policy options. The outcome of this set of choices is calculated using a "paper computer." Outcomes are revealed to players in the form of news bulletins. Each country team is then automatically referred to a brief programmed message or advice, and to a workbook page on which they plan the next move. Countries have strategic-information files, troops, and money (required to support troop action). After a team has planned its next action, a new informal negotiation session begins.

Life Career

Game available from Western Publishing Company.

Life Career is a simulation of certain features of the labor market, the education market, and the marriage market — as they now operate in the United States, and as projections indicate they will operate in the future. The purpose of the game is to give students an understanding of these institutions and some experience in planning for their own future. The game is for any number of teams of two to four players and lasts two to six hours.

Action. Teams of students act as the decision makers for a fictitious person, each team attempting to plan the most satisfying life for that person over an eight-year, or eight-round, period. The teams decide whether their person is going to stay in school or drop out, get a part-time or full-time job, get married, have children; they also decide how much time their person spends for leisure and family responsibilities. Any of the activities requires a certain investment of time, training, money, and so on, and a person clearly cannot engage in all the available activities. Thus the players' problem is to choose the combinations of activities that will, in their opinion, maximize the person's present satisfaction and his chances for a good life in the future.

Each team fills in a form showing a typical week's schedule during a year in the life of their person; this is given to a scorer, who computes points in four areas: education, occupation, family life, and leisure. The scorer's spinners and tables are based on recent U.S. census reports and other national survey data; these scoring aids indicate the probability of certain events occurring in a person's life, given his personal characteristics, past experiences, and present efforts.

Resource materials are available to the players to aid them in making their decisions; in using them, players become familiar with the format of job handbooks, school catalogs, want ads, and application forms.

Life Career was designed for high school and college students, and has been tested extensively at those levels. Nothing in the game would prevent its use at the junior high school level, however; it has been used with success, though with less depth of involvement, by students as young as sixth grade. Life Career has also been widely used by 4-H clubs, job-training centers, and other youth organizations outside of school.

Generation Gap

Game available from Western Publishing Company.

This simulation focuses on the interaction between a parent and an adolescent son or daughter when they disagree on certain issues. The conflict is presented within a context of rules that reflect the structure of power and interdependence in the family. The purpose is to generate some understanding of the structure and to shape effective strategies for handling the conflict. The game is designed for four to ten adolescents, and takes one-half to one hour.

Action. The game has several versions. The basic version concerns five issues, where the child has two behavior alternatives for each issue. One alternative (in terms of the scoring) is preferred by the player who has the parent's role, the other by the one who portrays the child. Each issue varies in its importance to the player. The parent's score is determined exclusively by the child's behavior (which the child indicates on the playing board); the child's score is determined jointly by his own behavior and by parental punishment, if any. Each round of the game starts with a few minutes' discussion between parent and child in which they may try to reach agreement on how the child will behave. On any issue where agreement is not reached, the parent gives an order to the child on how to behave. The child then selects his behavior; he may violate agreements, disobey orders, or both. The parent can, within certain constraints, supervise the behavior and punish the child (and subtract points from his score) if disobedience or violations of agreement are disclosed.

Parent and child do not compete against each other; a parent competes against other parents, and a child against other children, who are playing at the other boards.

Additional versions introduce parental rewards (rather than punishments), "temptations" of the child, barriers to intrafamily communication, happiness or tenseness of the family atmosphere, siblings, and other more complicated factors of parent-child relations.

Association

Game available from Western Publishing Company.

The Association game simulates social and psychological aspects of stratification—specifically, the tendency to associate with people of the same social class; the possibility of gaining or losing status by associating with social "superiors" or "inferiors"; and the deference required from the inferior in association with a superior. The game was designed for eight to ten college students and takes one to two hours.

Action. Each player is assigned to one of four social strata. In each round players may invite others to associate with them by exchanging markers. In associations between players in the same stratum, both players gain "balance points." A player who extensively associates with superiors (inferiors) becomes upward (downward) mobile; he gains (loses) mobility points, and plays the next round in a higher (lower) stratum. Players from the highest stratum, if they succeed in remaining in this stratum throughout the game, gain points. Players may offer deference points to each other to induce association (or may require deference points before accepting association); but explicit bargaining does not take place. Rejected invitations produce penalties of negative "embarrassment points."

In the advanced version, status of players is secret, but "styles of life" are defined for each social stratum. Players may attempt to present themselves as belonging to a different stratum (exhibiting a different life style) from their true one. Disclosing such deceit or being found out generates "one-upsmanship," "embarrassment points," and "vicarious embarrassment."

Consumer

Game available from Western Publishing Company.

This is a simulation of consumer buying in which players combine limited income with credit to purchase products they want and need. The game teaches the basic economics of budgeting income and of installment buying, and demonstrates the problems and opportunities involved in the use of credit. The Consumer game is for twelve to thirty-four players at high school level and takes from one and one-half to two and one-half hours.

Action. Most players are consumers who are trying to purchase certain products by using what they consider a wise buying strategy over eight "months." Each consumer receives a monthly income which he may spend or save as he chooses. The prices of the products remain generally constant. However, players receive satisfaction points (utility points) for each item purchased and, for most of these items, the utility points vary over the eight months according to a prearranged schedule. Thus the decision of when to buy the particular product, and whether or not it is worth going into debt for, becomes important. The buying period when an item is of greatest value may not coincide with the time when the consumer has the necessary amount of money. The occurrence of unplanned or random events in the game makes this especially likely. Thus a player may become unexpectedly unemployed and find it necessary to borrow money to purchase the products, pay a hospital bill, or pay off other installment debts. Consumers compete to maximize their utility points while minimizing credit or interest charges, for which they are penalized.

Other players in the game represent a bank, a finance company, and a department store from which the consumers may borrow money or arrange credit. These institutions compete against each other, receiving points for each transaction and losing points for debtors who prove bad risks.

The game is structured in such a way as to encourage players to set priorities—what they want and can afford to buy, when they can afford to buy, when it might be desirable to borrow money, from whom, and at which competitive rate of interest. They cope with credit ratings, contract negotiations, sales discounts, unanticipated events not generally covered by insurance.

Community Disaster

Game available from Western Publishing Company.

This game simulates a community hit by a localized natural disaster. The purpose of the game is to give players an understanding of the interrelationships of agencies, organizations, and individuals in a community at a time of a crisis, and to give them advance practice in coping with problems that arise. It is designed for six to twelve players at the high school or college level, and takes two to four hours.

Action. In the basic game each player is a member of the community represented on the central map, which gives the location of police stations, fire departments, industrial and residential areas, hospitals, and so forth, and the network of roads connecting them. At the outset of the game a disaster hits an unspecified part of town; people may be injured, property destroyed. Each player is given a role. He is an adult with spouse and children scattered in different parts of town, and he also is an important member of the community, holding a job that contributes to its welfare. His problem is to alleviate his anxiety for family and property, which may be located within the disaster area, while preventing anxiety from arising should he leave his job. He acts by listening to radio broadcasts; by telephoning relatives, friends, or agencies; by moving around the community, operating an agency, driving an ambulance. Each activity requires expenditure of "energy units," and clearly a person cannot do everything at once; he has to choose the combination of activities that he feels will most quickly locate the disaster area, evaluate the people he cares about, and overcome the disaster.

For example, to evacuate relatives in the disaster area means entering the area. This in turn requires the intervention of various agencies — the Department of Public Works must clear the roads, the Fire Department must control any blazes, the police must control road jams. If the community cannot organize itself quickly or efficiently enough, the disaster will spread, possibly causing damage beyond repair (in such a case everyone "loses").

At the end of a game, players elect — from among the three participants with the lowest total "anxiety" score — the one who did the most for the community. The winner, then, was both most efficient in committing his own energy and most visibly cooperative in helping his neighbors overcome the disaster.

There are two levels to the game. In the first, players cope with the disaster with no prior collective planning. In the second, having played the first game, players organize; they now can acquire training to operate agencies, install first-aid centers or duplicate agencies, agree on a plan of action in the event of a disaster. They then replay the disaster.

Raid

Game available from Games Central, Abt Associates, Inc.

Raid is a simple game used in teaching groups of disadvantaged students about the city crime problem and its possible solutions. The game requires twenty to forty high school students and lasts two hours.

Action. Specifically, the game consists of the interaction between a team of police, a team of racketeers, and teams representing city blocks. The police and racketeers have resources in the form of weapons and men. The city blocks have the resources of men and money. The objective of the police team is to catch the racketeers; the racketeers try to obtain money and recruit men from the city blocks. The city blocks seek to maintain or increase their wealth and their population. The police and racketeers may visit (raid) the city blocks at certain times, but otherwise all communications must be written.

Propaganda

Game available from Maret Company
or WFF 'N PROOF.®

The game's purpose is to teach children and adults to recognize propaganda techniques, as used by professionals in molding public opinion. It requires three to seven players in grade four or up.

Action. Over fifty techniques are presented, such as quotations out of context, bargaining appeal, attraction, a strawman, faulty analogy, and rationalization. Players analyze the writing of lawyers, politicians, advertisers, and others and try to separate the emotional appeal from the actual content of the idea. Two hundred forty examples are provided for

analysis. Each player labels each example, basing his judgment on given definitions of technique. After the decisions are tallied, players find they are either popular voters (that is, they are in the majority), or minority voters. Each of the minority voters, if any, then has a choice of:
1. accepting the popular vote
2. challenging the popular voters
3. trying to persuade the popular voters to change their minds
Points can be won by accurate labeling, correct challenging, or effective persuading. Later, players provide their own examples from newspapers, television, magazines, and political speeches, and play the expert's game.

Plans

Game available from Simile II.

Pressure groups, their influence on federal legislation, and consequent changes in the national economy are studied in this simulation. Its objective is to give high school students an understanding of how special-interest groups function in the United States.

Action. The students are divided into six interest groups: military, civil rights, nationalists, internationalists, business, and labor. The members of each interest group discuss the fifteen policies presented in the game. The group must decide how to allocate its influence so as to further the policies it favors; at the same time, it must block the adoption of policies it believes would be harmful to society. Changes in society are made known through changes in eighteen national indicators. These indicators are affected by policy and also by national trends in society. The effects of adopting particular strategies are calculated and the results given back to the groups.

Groups receive information through descriptions of the current state of affairs, and a statistical summary; messages may be sent between groups as well as requests for conferences. The policies explored are topical, realistic problems of the United States. For example, Policy 5 is "Federal aid to education should be increased by $3 billion"; Policy 2, "The maximum corporate income tax rate should be reduced from 48% to 40%."

The interest group's goal is to get a policy adopted; players do not know how many influence "units" this requires, however, and must use successive periods to learn the policy's sensitivity to pressure.

The game requires high-level skills in analyzing data, making predictions concerning the nature and direction of social change, estimating how other groups will act, and adopting appropriate negotiating strategies. Information from period one is a useful guide in period two, and so on in successive periods; thus the game has an evolving structure that makes the total simulation complete and rich with possibilities.

Section

Game available from The Macmillan Company.

The game deals with conflicts of interests among sections of a political territory; it explores the molding of these conflicts by economic interests, and their expression in the political process. The game of Section is designed for high school students.

Action. Students play the roles of citizens of a hypothetical state, Midland, U.S.A. It is composed of four sections — agricultural, prosperous industrial, declining industrial, and underdeveloped rural. There is a capital city as well. Each sectional team desires state aid for pet projects, and each individual prefers those projects that will benefit him most.

The game is set on the eve of an election. Basic characteristics of the state are conveyed in newspaper articles, and individual interests are delineated in profiles.

The game proceeds through a number of stages. First, negotiations within sections indicate conflicts over the desirability of various enumerated projects. Progressive farmers want state aid for an agricultural college, for example, and conservative farmers don't want the state involved in anything. Then players negotiate across the state in order to identify coincident interest with individuals in other sections. For example, a farmer who wants a road built to the prosperous industrial section may find more support there than in his own section. Students then return to sectional teams to draft a proposal to the state legislature, in cooperation with their representatives. These negotiate with an executive commitee to allocate the state budget, subject to the approval of their constituents.

Finally, political sanctions are applied in the form of reelecting or ousting the political representatives. Scoring for the game contains three steps. Citizens vote on whether their representatives remain in office. At the same time, representatives vote on whether executive committee members keep their positions. Then, the approved budget is analyzed to see which section received the greatest number of benefits. The total of these three scores for each sectional team determines the winning team.

Napoli

Information available from Simile II.

Napoli simulates the legislative process in the context of the two-party system of the United States. The game also gives practice in political negotiations, and exposes the players to the cross-pressures from party and constituency as well as from speeches, negotiations, and lobbies. The players are divided into eight groups of about four players each. The game is suitable for junior and senior high school students.

Action. The students are assigned to one of two political parties, one being liberal and the other conservative. They are also assigned to a geographical region. The goal of the game is to get reelected, which is done by passing legislation favorable to your region and to your party. Each participant's probability of reelection is evaluated on the basis of his performance.

The game begins when players participate in party caucuses and elect officers. They proceed to regional caucuses and then to the first legislative session. The legislative body elects a speaker and votes on proposed bills. Speeches and negotiations take place before the vote. After four bills have been voted on, the players are told of their chances for reelection and the cycle begins again.

Steam

Information available from Abt Associates, Inc.

The game deals with coal mining and steam engines, and their interrelationships in nineteenth century England. There are two versions, one complex and the other simplified. Either version calls for a group of five players.

Simplified Version. The players are mine owners competing for profits by selling their coal to a referee. Each tries to maximize his profit by selling coal at the highest price, and extracting it at the lowest cost. The game proceeds in sessions called bidding rounds. The mine owners prepare bid forms that are checked by the referee. The game proceeds for eight to thirteen bidding rounds; at the end, the mine owners fill out a final balance sheet.

Complex Version. The class engages in a simulation of smelting iron, buying and selling wood and coal for smelting, introducing steam pumps to pump seepage from coal mines. The class is divided into teams of iron mill owners, coal mine operators, and inventors. The players learn to make business decisions under changing market and technological conditions, and learn the impact of economics on technological innovations.

Revolution

Information available from Abt Associates, Inc.

Revolution was designed as the central element in a junior high school unit on the English Civil War; it focuses on factors contributing to that conflict. Twenty to forty students play the game, which requires approximately five hours to play.

Action. Players receive brief profiles of real historical characters. Most represent members of Parliament with Puritan and Parliamentary sympathies. King Charles and his advisers and tax collectors are also included.

The players do not know that two teams are created in the game, since Parliamentarians and Royalists have been given different rules. The basic objective of King Charles is to obtain enough money to keep his government going without calling Parliament. (This sum is indicated in his profile.) The objective of the merchants and gentlemen is to maximize their wealth and uphold their religious principles.

In the course of the game, players are confronted by tax collectors and religious agents of the king. If they refuse to pay or comply with religious requirements, they are brought to court and possibly sent to jail. If they do comply, they lose money and religious points.

Throughout the game, new events are announced through news bulletins. The final one states that the Scots have invaded England and are demanding £800 per day from the king. The game is rigged to guarantee that King Charles cannot raise this sum of money without calling Parliament. When he does, players have a chance to air their grievances and make demands on the king in return for money. In a sense, King Charles is the implied loser. But the major purpose of the game is to give students an understanding of the opposed points of view of the protagonists and to simulate some of the frustration Englishmen experienced when legal channels for redress of grievances were shut off.

Simplified Version. At this level, individual role playing is not required. Instead, teams of merchants and gentlemen, with varying religious sympathies, receive a group profile and respond as a group to events introduced in news bulletins. After each news bulletin, six students are selected to place a colored strip of paper on a chart under "King" or "Parliament" to indicate shifting loyalties. At first, the bulk of the population remains uncommitted, but as grievances build up, more and more students take sides. The strips of paper are color coded so that ultimately a socioeconomic chart is created.

Empire

Game available from KDI Instructional Systems

The game demonstrates the place of the American colonists in the British Empire, and how their membership in the empire affected the way they made their living. Empire is played by seven teams and takes three to five hours; it was designed for the junior high school level.

Action. Players are divided into seven teams, which include London merchants, colonial farmers, and British West Indies planters. Each team starts the game with goods to sell and consumer demands to be met. In each move the players bargain over prices, buy and sell goods, and move ships across the Atlantic. Certain goods are put into special classes and smuggling is a possible strategy with rewards and punishments.

During the game, players encounter a London monopoly, arbitrary trade laws, the risks of smuggling and piracy, the Royal Navy as protector or law enforcer, and other phenomena of the colonial empire.

The Slave Trade Game

Information available from Abt Associates, Inc.

The game dramatizes the varieties of misery suffered by Negroes in the eighteenth century when they were transported as slaves. Designed for the junior high school level, it is meant to be a supplement to Empire. Playing time is one hour.

Action. The object of the game is to survive. Some of the life-destroying experiences suffered by the Negro slaves are presented. Many Negro slaves perish, and few of the players survive to the end of the game. In the course of the game the players receive situation cards that either kill them off, or inform them that they have been sold to a planter. The survival of the players who go to plantations is also determined by situation cards. The winner, chosen from the survivers, is the player who is the most cheerful, patient, and obedient to the end. This rule is kept secret until the end, and then explained.

Adventuring

Information available from Abt Associates, Inc.

Adventuring helps junior high school students develop an understanding of the social structure of seventeenth century England, preliminary to their study of the English Civil War. The game calls for three teams of three players each.

Action. The game attempts to demonstrate the reasons and the opportunities for social mobility of the most mobile portion of the population — the yeomen, gentry, and merchant groups. The gameboard consists of a three-dimensional pyramid. Each social class starts at a different level. Each player is given money and land. Each has a family of three sons and must choose a career for each of them. In this manner, yeomen may become farmers or tradesmen, merchants may become lawyers, and so on.

Each career requires an investment of money or land or both. The player must choose between those careers with little initial training but small future rewards, and those that require investment but offer great rewards. Acting simultaneously, the players each allocate three tokens, representing three sons, to a place on the game pyramid. The basic goals are upward movement and acquiring more wealth and influence. Downward movement is possible through bad luck or mismanagement of resources. Movement between classes is possible by buying land or by marriage. The student thus has an opportunity to plan the best strategy for social climbing while dealing with various social and political forces.

Manchester

Information available from Abt Associates, Inc.

The game is intended as part of a curriculum unit on the Industrial Revolution in England, for students in grades ten to twelve. It focuses on the economic forces behind the migration of workers from the country to the city. The game is played by seven players around a board, and takes at least two hours.

Action. Students are given the roles of squire, farmer, mill owner, and laborer. They sit around a board depicting a village with plots of land, a city with two factories, and a poorhouse. The players are given resources in the form of money or land, the object being to maximize wealth. The mill owner, for example, starts with a one-man machine; he is given a schedule showing the costs and possible outputs of mill machines. He makes decisions about how much cloth to produce, and at what price to sell it. He also bargains with the laborers for wages.

The laborers receive wages, and have to make bargains with the mill owner or squire. All the players pay subsistence costs to the bank, and defaulters go to the poorhouse. Laborers tend to move from the village to the city as the mill owners invest in more machines and require more workers. In this way, the simulation replicates the economic forces operating at the time of the Industrial Revolution.

Galápagos

Information available from Abt Associates, Inc.

Factors involved in the evolution of species are studied in the game of Galápagos. The game is designed for the high school level, and requires four to eight players.

Action. The game is played around a map board representing the Galápagos Islands, where Darwin made his observations of finches. Wind patterns, geological strata, and food supplies are shown. Players assume the roles of scientists and are asked to predict the path of speciation. Birds are differentiated by food-gathering abilities as indicated by beak types. The kind of food available on different islands changes over time, and the birds are supposed to be in competition for the available food supply. Birds migrate and adapt to the food supply. Players are asked to predict evolutionary patterns in the future, although they are made to understand that Darwin analyzed past, rather than future development.

Machinist

Information available from Information Systems for Vocational Decisions, Graduate School of Education, Harvard University.

The game's purpose is to enable junior and senior high school students to consider realistically a possible career as a machinist. The game attempts to lead students to make effective vocational decisions based on information contained in the game, as well as on other investigations they are motivated to make as a result of playing. In making one complete play, a student learns the work opportunities, risks, and benefits of making different job choices that may come up in the twenty years after leaving high school.

Although designed primarily for a single player, Machinist can be readily modified for play by five or six students. Two or three hours are required for play.

Action. As currently designed, the game uses puzzle pieces to represent important stages in the player's machining career, years spent in any one stage, and reasons why the player moved from one stage to the next. Each year, or round, the student makes a decision about the relative rewards of earning more money by working overtime, or of having more leisure time to spend with his family. Each year he also acquires more experience or training, and increases his chances of getting promoted. The probability of being promoted is determined by ability, experience, and location in a union or a nonunion shop. At each career stage, the player receives information that describes his current work and announces his opportunities for his next job. At the end of the game the player can see the overall pattern of his career, as depicted by a puzzle he constructed and by charts showing how much leisure time and income he had each year. The win criteria are determined by the career goals that the student set for himself and the extent to which he achieved them by the end of the game. If more than one person plays there is direct competition for jobs; win criteria are then based on achieving career goals first.

Computer Games

Computer games are in an early stage of development. The machine acts as either the opponent or the referee for one individual. If a student plays tick-tack-toe against the computer, for example, the machine acts as his opponent and will use the strategies human players ordinarily employ to tie or defeat the other player. If the player is simulating an economic planner, in contrast, the computer will not try to defeat him by undermining his plans; instead it will evaluate strategies and advise him as to how well he has done.

The student sits at a teletype machine or typewriting console, which is connected to a computer. Messages from the computer are typed out on the paper in the typewriter: "How many dollars do you wish to spend this month on entertainment?" The player types in his answer — for example, "50" — which is transmitted to the computer. The stored logical program in the computer takes the player's answers and determines the consequences of his decision: "You can't meet your car payments this month; the finance company takes your car away. You now have to take the bus to work and this costs thirty cents each working day." After the results of his decisions are reported to the player, he usually has a chance to reflect on the results and change his decision. He may decide to reduce his entertainment budget to $10, for example.

In summary, a computer game operates as follows: The computer asks the player questions. The player then answers, basing his decision on some reasoning or strategic process, though admittedly his first responses might be random. The results of the decision are then reported to the player, or a new situation is described. The player may, at this point, be given clues or hints that will encourage him to develop better ways of dealing with the situation presented in the game. The cycle is then repeated, with the computer asking the player questions.

The use of computer games is limited at present, not only because schools do not have the required equipment, but because the alternatives available to the player are limited, and generally presented in the form of multiple-choice questions. Desirable negotiations and broad policy decisions are seldom presented in computer games.

Interaction with other players, a key factor in most manual games, is limited in computer games — except where the computer merely serves as a calculator for complex mathematical computations in a manual game. The unplanned situation, which can arise in a manual game, usually cannot be handled well in a computer game. Nor are qualitative variables processed well. Thus the range of communication between player and machine is limited.

Computer games and manual games are, however, similar in some respects. In both, players have objectives and strive to achieve them. In both, they have resources and constraints on what they can do. Their actions result in altered environmental situations. At present, however, it appears that manual games can accomplish more at less cost than computer games.

Some examples of computer games follow.

Sumerian

Information available from the Board of Cooperative Educational Services.

The game is a computer model of the ancient Sumerian civilization; it is used to teach basic economic principles to sixth-grade students. Settled farming, specialized crafts, and foreign trade develop as the result of the student's allocation of scarce resources and his response to innovation and disaster. As the ruler of a central economy, the student determines the production, savings, and investment quotas. If he is to achieve his objective of a growing economy, he must evaluate his present consumption requirements and his potential for future development in deciding these quotas. The Sumerian game is played by one student at a computer console that feeds back progress reports and chance situations in response to student decisions.

Action. The student is introduced to the Sumerian civilization with a tape and slide presentation. The game is then played in three phases. At each phase the student is told the resources he has available and the population of the country. In the first phase of play, as Luduga I, the ruler of an agricultural economy, the student must allocate his grain harvest among food for his people, seed for next year's planting, and inventory for future needs. In the second phase, as Luduga II, he has the opportunity to apply surplus grain to the development of crafts. In the third phase, trade and more complex problems are introduced. Throughout the simulation the student must respond to disasters and technological innovations, which are programmed to appear in a random manner. In a good game, the student will find the population of his country growing and the harvest increasing. In a poor game, there will be a decrease of population or harvest or both.

Free Enterprise

Information available from the Board of Cooperative Educational Services.

The game gives the student an understanding of economic principles as they operate under a system of free enterprise. It takes one student fifteen to thirty hours to complete the play; a 1401 computer is used.

Action. The game consists of two phases which, although intended to be played sequentially, may be used as two distinctly separate games. In the first phase of the game (Toy Town) the player assumes the role of the owner and operator of a small toy store. By using the opportunities provided in the simulated environment, and by making decisions to combat those factors in the environment that would be detrimental to the operation of his small business, the player should be able to increase the sales and net worth of his store. In the second phase of the game the player assumes the role of the owner of a firm that maufactures surfboards. If this segment of the game is played in conjunction with the first phase, the transition from sales to production is necessitated by market saturation for toys and allied products, which forces the player to diversify his interests to include a manufacturing operation. Or, more simply, the costs involved in further increasing the size of his retail operation are such that his money could be more profitably spent in another endeavor.

CHAPTER 4

THE ROLE OF THE TEACHER

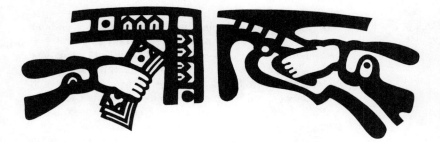

4

Administering Games

The Teacher as Coach

Debriefing the Game

It is scarcely to be expected that innovations in education will leave the teacher's traditional role unaltered. Whether manifested in the "discovery" method, the computer medium, or the "ungraded subjects" philosophy, the trend of current educational development is toward increased interaction between the student and curriculum materials, and the student and his peers. In exploiting students' ability to learn from each other, in encouraging curiosity and free inquiry, in removing the threat of punishment by low grades, in allowing the student to learn at his own pace by the use of new technology, the traditional dominance of the teacher in the classroom is slowly being whittled away.

Even if the teacher lectures less, his importance is undiminished. For classic proof of this, one has only to examine the use of films in the classroom. As a medium film totally replaces the teacher for a portion of the school day. But that portion of the day is likely to be wasted unless the teacher discusses the film afterward and integrates it into the rest of the curriculum.

While students may learn from each other, or from a computer, or by making mistakes on the way to discovery, nobody has yet suggested that the teacher is incidental to the learning process. What is implicit in new educational methods is the attempt to allow the student to deal directly with instructional materials, with the teacher acting as aid, rather than judge.

In educational games, the teacher's altered role beomes obvious. While students play among themselves, the teacher serves as coach and referee. In this situation, the teacher's superior knowledge is perceived as a tool to help students to perform better—to achieve their objectives in the game—and not as a threatening standard that students must meet, or suffer failure.

Administering Games

The Teacher's Homework

Nobody likes to be caught short but nobody, including the designers, can account for all the possible events and questions that might arise in the course of playing an educational game. If flexibility is one of the key advantages of the medium, how can the teacher adequately prepare to use a game?

In the ideal situation, a group of teachers would play the game first to become familiar with the range of possible courses of action and the general operation of the game. In many cases, this is not at all burdensome. The author participated in a test play of the game of Pollution with fifteen teachers, some of whom planned to use the game with their classes; the test play lasted an evening. But it is not always possible to devote the time or gather the participants to play a game from beginning to end, especially when the game is designed for thirty players and four or five hours of playing time.

Short of actually playing a game, the teacher can become familiar with it by "walking through" it, that is, acquainting himself with the game materials (gameboard, play money, chance cards, or profiles and scenario) and the rules. In the case of a gameboard, familiarity can be acquired in the course of arranging the materials before class.

To facilitate the teacher's preparation, special materials usually accompany educational games. These materials include essays describing what the game is designed to teach; often what the game is *not* meant to accomplish is discussed as well. When simplifications in a process have been made for purposes of making a game more playable, these are indicated. The actors in the game, whether teams or individuals, are described and the resources of each player are listed to aid the teacher in assigning roles and distributing resources. The kinds of activities that the game requires or produces are usually described; this helps the teacher develop a feel for the action before the game is actually played.

The teacher materials also indicate how the class should be arranged, where the boards, if any, should be placed, how much time should be allotted to any activity and to the game as a whole. In addition, suggestions for postgame discussion are included, which the teacher can use and build on as he sees fit. It is also advisable for the teacher to read the instructions provided for the student. These are usually very brief, for the student is rarely told what to expect. Most useful is the skeletal outline, or agenda of activities, that summarizes the action of the game. An example of the outline of a cycle might be:

1. Decide what goods you will produce.
2. Pay the costs of production and receive goods.
3. Sell goods to consumers.
4. Buy goods you need.

With this brief list well in mind, the teacher may then refer to the detailed description of how to execute these actions as needed.

In role-play games, where the materials consist of a unique profile for each player, the teacher materials summarize the basic list of actors and their objectives in the game; the teacher need not read and try to remember each profile beforehand.

Materials for the teacher and rules for the student tend to run twenty typewritten pages or less. The amount of time needed for studying them will vary. For example, eighteen teachers responded to questionnaires about their use of the role-play game called Section. Eight teachers estimated that their preparation took more time than average for a comparable period of classroom activity (five to six classroom hours); four estimated it required less preparation, and six stated that preparation time for the game was the same as for other activities. The responses are difficult to evaluate. Preparation time varied from forty minutes, which one teacher judged to be more than average, to five hours, which another teacher judged to be less. On the basis of very limited information, the author can only conclude that the preparation time for educational games does not seem to be significantly longer than for other classroom activities. It may be more concentrated, however, since getting ready to launch a game means preparing for three to five class periods at one time.

Preparing the Class

It is advisable to prepare the class the day before beginning a game by giving a copy of the rules to each student; for a role-play game, copies of the scenario and the individual profiles should be distributed also. If students become familiar with the rules and their roles beforehand, the game is likely to begin more easily. Unfortunately, the rules of any game, educational or entertainment, are difficult to understand before they are actually used. One learns the rules of a game, not by reading them, but by playing. For that reason, students who have failed to learn the rules at home should not be penalized. Testing the student on his homework, in this case, would be both unfair and damaging to the ethos of game play.

Roles and Players

Casting Roles. The nature of roles varies from game to game. In some, there is little differentiation between roles; all the students might play the role of merchants, for example. In other games, however, roles may vary in the degree of activity and aggressiveness they require. A small number of students may play political leaders and the rest may play ordinary citizens.

In the latter case, the casting problem arises. Should the teacher assign the most aggressive roles to the most aggressive students?

Among teachers using educational games, practice varies from choosing numbers in a hat, to asking for volunteers, to assigning roles randomly, to deliberately assigning leadership roles to those who are natural leaders in the class. Deliberate casting has the advantage of avoiding the potential delays and uncertainty of a student playing a role he may not be able to handle. On the other hand, natural leaders are likely to make any role they play an aggressive one, sometimes with interesting results in the game.

It is suggested that students who do not perform well in conventional classroom activities by given a chance to play outstanding roles, if they are interested. In a class that uses games regularly, this practice can be altered if it is not successful. If the teacher decides to cast a role-play game, examination of all the roles is necessary to determine which students would be appropriate for each.

Some games require the marginal function of banker to distribute and collect money. Again, it is suggested that slower students should not be assigned automatically and consistently to this low-level role. Students should be asked to take turns playing banker and if nobody really wants to, the banking function can be combined with a more active role in the game. Some games are designed to be played more than once as part of a curriculum. In such cases, students should play different roles to gain a better understanding of the process under study.

Number of Players. Most role-play games are designed for an entire class, or approximately thirty players. Teacher materials will indicate which roles may be omitted if the class is smaller than average, and include additional roles in case the class is larger. If the class is too small to provide the minimum number of players to make the game work, two small classes may be combined.

Board games are usually planned for smaller numbers of players. If a board game is designed for a full class, the board is likely to be presented in several pieces that can be arranged in different parts of the room to prevent crowding. Some board games work best when played by ten or fifteen students; in a large class, two or three such games can be successfully operated simultaneously.

If this arrangement is used in a class of diverse ability, each group should have a mixture of abilities. If the best students are assigned to one game and the slowest to another, the opportunity for slower students to learn from brighter ones is lost; such division is also likely to discourage slower students, who may play the game with less initial ease than the brighter group. The principle of mixing slower and brighter students applies as well to the makeup of teams when the entire class participates in one game.

In-class Briefing

Before play begins, the teacher should brief the class on what the game is about and review the basic outline of the rules. This briefing should, by definition, be *brief*. A long, tedious discussion of every detail of the rules would be the easiest way to suffocate the students' motivation to play the game.

An optimum briefing runs approximately fifteen minutes, and covers the following items:
1. The problem that the game poses to the players.
2. The actors in the game and their objectives.
3. The physical layout of the game — whether this involves the arrangement of gameboards or the assignment of locations in the room to represent geographical areas.
4. A demonstration of the "first move" in the game.
    a. In a board game, a member of each team would make the appropriate move, such as shifting a piece on the board, so that the others may see how to begin play.
    b. In a role-play game, a script for a typical negotiation sequence is sometimes provided. If a few students read from this script, the types of issues and arguments involved can be made clear. If no demonstration script is provided, the sequence of negotiations should be described and outlined on the board. For example: "Teams A and B, and teams C and D negotiate for fifteen minutes. Then teams A and C, and teams B and D meet for fifteen minutes."

A broad overview of the actors is useful, eliminating uncertainty about the personnel of the game. Individual players can describe their roles and objectives; or a spokesman from each team can give this information. Again, this preliminary should be kept very brief.

The purpose of the briefing is, basically, to get students started in the game. Specific questions about rules and procedures can be resolved as they arise in the course of play.

Supervising the Play

Handling Questions. No one can be expected to memorize the complete operation of a game before playing it. If this is so, how can the teacher realistically hope to answer every question that arises during the game? The question itself betrays the assumptions most of us have about the role of the teacher. If we expect and insist that the teacher always have all the answers in all classroom situations, educational games cannot be utilized to maximum advantage; the teacher would be too prone to constrain the students' strategies and imagination within the strict limits of the rules of the game.

Individual teaching styles will determine the manner in which any game is used; but if the expectation of knowing all the answers is removed, greater flexibility of approach can be achieved. One basic purpose of educational games is, after all, to allow the student to participate freely in the issues and processes under study. There would be no justification for using games if the teacher's objective was simply to convey a set of facts.

The teacher should not hesitate to seek answers to questions through discussion with the students. Delays would be prevented if the teacher responded directly to the simple procedural question of "what to do next." But the problematic questions, with no answers in the rules, could be settled mutually. In an economics game, for example, a player might ask "Am I allowed to sell my machinery?" This question raises other questions, which the class can discuss. Would it be realistic to sell the machinery? Would other players want to buy it? Why does the player want to sell? If the machinery is outdated or inefficient, why would anyone want it? If the sale of machinery is permitted, what price should be asked relative to the initial price and to prices of other items in the game?

As a result of this discussion, students and teacher might come to a conclusion: Outdated machinery does not attract a buyer; however, players ought to be allowed to sell it to the bank at-a loss, as a means of acquiring capital for investment in equipment that is more modern and productive. On the other hand, the class might decide, for game purposes, to leave out the option of selling equipment—even though a businessman in the real world would not necessarily be stuck with owning old equipment.

In a test play of Section (in which citizens of different sections of a hypothetical state negotiate for state funds for pet projects), actors came up with their own suggestions for projects, such as an airport. The students' own ideas were easily incorporated into the list of possible projects, once all the implications of such variants were examined. What should an airport cost relative to the cost of other projects in the game? Besides the section that proposed the airport, what other sections or individuals are likely to support it? Oppose it? What are the arguments for and against an airport? In terms of scoring the game (based on the number and kinds of projects each section manages to get), how should a section be rewarded if it gets funds for an airport?

A suggestion like the airport proposal reflects the players' basic understanding of the game and their ability to go beyond it. Such initiative should be encouraged. Not all the questions raised in a game need to be answered immediately. The teacher might assign students to research a question or prepare an argument in favor of making a proposed change.

In playing the game of Pollution, some elementary students in Wellesley, Massachusetts decided to improve on what the designers had done. The first phase of the game is a simulation of the economy of a town. In the course of producing goods and services, students also increase air and water pollution. The game proceeds with the use of demand cards indicating the production volume of various factories, the amount of money earned by the manufacturer, and a corresponding amount of pollution. Students felt that the salaries for various producers in the community did not vary enough, and that the demand cards were not interesting enough. To the designers' pleasure, rather than embarrassment, the players wrote their own demand cards and improved the game.

In some cases, the types of questions that arise reflect the students' understanding or intuition of the simplifications that the designer has intentionally made. For example, in a game involving international trade, students may ask why they don't have to wait, that is, simulate time, in crossing the ocean to trade their goods. The teacher may choose to explain that the factor of time was eliminated so that players would not become bored during inactive periods; or he may solicit suggestions as to how waiting time could be incorporated, and try a cycle in the new way. If the new version works well, and the students prefer it, why not modify the game? (In this particular case, however, the students are likely to see that boredom is the price for verisimilitude.)

What to Do During Board Games. What is the teacher likely to be doing while students are playing a game? If it is a board game, with one board for the entire class, the teacher should be an observer, at hand to respond to questions, to volunteer suggestions, and possibly to perform the function of banker so that all the students may participate in the more active roles. While students are deeply involved in the action of the game, the teacher functions as a coach; he is available "on the bench" for aid and encouragement, but not actively participating.

When several groups are playing the same game simultaneously, the teacher should circulate among the groups and observe the action; he should offer help when students seem to be uncertain as to what to do, or when they do not seem to be playing the game as well as those in other groups. When questions arise in this situation, the teacher may choose to deal directly with the particular group; or he may address the group's question to the class at large, so that students may benefit from the solutions and suggestions of their classmates.

Observing Role-play Games. In role-play games, where no gameboards are used, the teacher circulates throughout the class; he listens to negotiations among teams and individuals, offers suggestions where they seem needed, and moves on when a discussion seems to be going well.

Most role-play games require that the teacher keep track of time spent on each phase of negotiation, and that he announce the end of one phase and the beginning of the next. This time-keeping is unobtrusive and facilitates action.

What should the teacher do if he overhears a poor argument, or perhaps an incorrect one? In most cases, the teacher can rely on the fact that players' judgment of an argument is intrinsic to the game. A poor argument is likely to be perceived as such by other students, and hence will be unconvincing. Similarly, incorrect assertions — which are especially likely to occur in historical games — might be rebutted as play proceeds; if not, the opportunity to discuss anachronistic assumptions or errors of fact is presented in the postgame discussion. Certainly, the teacher ought not seize on overheard errors during play merely to try to keep all the facts straight. If all the teacher wishes to do is convey correct facts, there would be no need to use a game. But where understanding of a process is the primary objective, errors of fact can be overlooked and corrected later.

Activity Level

There is no doubt that the activity level in the classroom is higher during game play than in the lecture or question-answer situation. But as one enthusiastic teacher remarked, after a highly successful game, "What is too noisy? If the students learn when it's noisy, let's have more noise. . . ."

If the teacher can tolerate having many students moving around and talking, a higher activity level simply implies greater difficulty in keeping track of what is going on in the classroom. If games are used in the flexible way intended, the teacher simply cannot know everything that is happening in the course of play. For successful operation of the game, it is sufficient that the teacher circulate among the players. Then the multitude of events that occurred simultaneously in the game will be revealed to both teacher and students in the postgame discussion, or debriefing. Exploring together makes the game experience a truly cooperative effort, with the teacher in the nonthreatening position of coach instead of judge.

Modifying Games

An optional, but key, role the teacher can play is that of adapting or designing educational games. Given the limited availability of games now—and the likelihood that even when abundant, they may not be suited to every particular need—the teacher will find it profitable to explore the possibility of tailoring his own game materials. (See Chapter 5 for a how-to-do-it discussion of design and adaptation.)

A Summing Up

1. If possible, play the game through with other teachers or friends.
2. Become acquainted with the physical components of the game.
3. Thoroughly read the materials provided for the teacher's use.
4. Modify the game, if necessary, to meet particular needs of the class.
5. Decide the basis on which roles will be assigned. Try to include bright and slow students on the same teams.
6. Distribute copies of the rules, and profiles and scenarios where they are used, to each student the day before play.
7. Arrange the components of the game in the classroom.
8. Brief students on
   a. the purpose of the game
   b. the roles of individuals or teams, and objectives
   c. the physical layout of room
   d. the first move

This phase should not exceed fifteen minutes.

9. During play circulate among groups or individuals and offer suggestions where desirable, answer questions when necessary. Try to involve the student in answering his own questions and arriving at solutions.

The Teacher as Coach

Educational games alter the function of the teacher. They bypass the teacher's mediation between students and materials by requiring that players interact directly with the materials. They also contradict a fundamental part of the teacher's traditional role, for there are no right answers in a game. Consequently, it is not the teacher's function to judge the student's progress toward learning the facts, or to steer him clear of the pitfalls of error and oversight. A game provides no simple record of the information embodied in it to be used for testing or drilling students. Nor are solutions that are methodically derived rewarded at the expense of equally workable solutions arrived at intuitively. How different this is from the practice of grading test performance, particularly in mathematics, on the method of solution as well as the correctness of the answer. The problems that games present are usually too complex to make accidental winning likely, and adjustment for the possibility of a student arriving at the right answer in the wrong way is not necessary.

Games incorporate their own evaluation mechanism and reward system in the scoring and, in some cases, in the opportunity for players to judge the strategies of other players during play. The game, not the teacher, evaluates successful and unsuccessful play and rewards it accordingly.

This characteristic of educational games has its analogy in athletic contests. A team's coach can encourage and advise during play, and evaluate the strategy afterward. But evaluation of the team's performance is an intrinsic part of the game; the players win or lose. The coach's evaluation is important, but not for determining the outcome of the game — with the judgment of right and wrong that that implies. Rather, he aids in examining what the game has revealed to be good and poor play, so that players may profit from good and bad strategy in the future. But then no particular strategy is foolproof for all situations; success may depend on changing conditions, part of which is the strategy of the opposing team.

In such an open-ended situation, there are no simple criteria for making judgments. The teacher's function, then, becomes one of encouraging questioning and experimentation and helping students become comfortable with uncertainty. Specifically, the student must learn to cope with variations in conditions, accept the difficulty of perceiving all variables, make decisions despite the impossibility of controlling all variables, and hence accept variations in the degree of success achieved when dealing with those variables. In using text materials, a student may learn to handle the data presented and to expect a consistent level of success when tested. In a game, this student may find that he cannot hope to control the data, and he may experience vastly different results in two plays of the same game. If the former situation is more comfortable, the latter has realism to recommend it.

How does the teacher help students to accept uncertainty and open-ended systems? Only by accepting these facts himself. Few adults, after all, would deny that they accept and allow for variables in their lives. And most educators would defer to the notion that realities ought to be presented in the classroom to avoid producing cynicism in students. But the implications for teaching with educational games and other flexible media run counter to the most basic assumptions on which the school system is built.

The entire structure implies hierarchy and authority, closed systems, absolute standards of right and wrong. The teacher, older and wiser, is traditionally perceived as judge of right and wrong. The textbook appears as the repository of truth, partly because it has the aspect of a tidy package unblemished by loose ends and partly because it has been used as an absolute standard. The author is not denigrating the value of teacher or textbook, the most important resources in education. But the tradition of authority is so deeply ingrained in students as well as in teachers that change in the teacher's role may in fact prove to be more difficult to accept and effect than common sense would lead one to believe.

Adjusting to a New Role

For the sake of brevity, the author is trapped into setting out a tidy list of suggestions for acting in the altered role required by educational games. Exaggeration of the difficulty of adjusting to the change will be forgiven, it is hoped, as simply a means of underscoring the importance of the teacher's role.

The key is willpower.

1. Resist the temptation to correct minor errors.
2. Resist the temptation to offer a better strategy that the student does not perceive.
3. Resist the temptation to test or review, in minute detail, students' understanding of the rules or roles of the game.
4. Resist the temptation to correct any elaboration or alteration of the rules of the game.
5. Resist the temptation to keep perfect order. The noise level produced by thirty students talking at the same time need not exceed human tolerance.
6. Resist the temptation to stymie any points that seem to be irrelevant to the discussion. They often prove to be relevant; at worst, they will be brief digressions.
7. Resist the temptation to constrain the moderate physical movement a game may require.
8. Resist the temptation to answer students' questions about the game with "That's not in the rules."
9. Resist the temptation to avoid admitting lack of knowledge about a point of the game's operation or an aspect of the process under study.
10. Resist the temptation to consider a game a less serious form of education than a textbook.

Flexible use of games can encourage independent thinking and decision making in the direction of satisfying egalitarian ideals.

Should the Teacher Play the Game?

If educational games lessen the distance between teacher and student, should the teacher decrease that distance even further by actually participating in a game? This largely depends on the preference of the teacher. In the author's experience, however, some games lend themselves to teacher participation better than others.

On the whole, board games do not offer the teacher useful roles to play. The function of banker may sometimes be performed by the teacher to facilitate play and free a student for a more active role; or it may simply prove convenient for the teacher to handle money in the game while being available for questions and suggestions. With a game that requires several boards or more than one set of game materials, the teacher obviously should be free to circulate among the players and ought not be tied to any "housekeeping" function.

In role-play games, however, the teacher often has an opportunity to take part in the activity. It is not recommended that the teacher play as an ordinary member of any student team. Rather, some games provide for a single leader to organize debate and lead the discussion. These would tend to be simulations of legislative bodies where, for example, students play congressmen and the teacher could play the Speaker of the House.

In one exercise, junior high school students played members of Parliament arguing the advantages and disadvantages of colonization in the new world. The teacher played the role of Queen Elizabeth I, whom the students had to persuade to their point of view. This role gave the teacher the opportunity to control debate within the realistic context of parliamentary procedure and the institution of royalty. Students knew that if they displeased the queen by arguing too vehemently or by being impolite to players who disagreed with them they would probably lose influence with the queen.

In another simulation, students play the roles of delegates to the Continental Congresses, which met between 1774 and 1776. The teacher is encouraged to play the role of the president of the congress; this gives him the opportunity to moderate debate, and to lead students through a complex agenda of issues for discussion. In this, as in the previous exercise, the teacher can run the game from within its own framework, rather than intrude from the outside and threaten its magic spell. The teacher neither judges the students nor operates on an equal level with them, and the compromise seems to be highly successful. The teacher, of course, always has the option of assigning a role of leadership to an able student.

Debriefing the Game

One function that the teacher should neither delegate nor neglect is the debriefing. This is simply a postgame discussion, but the value of a game is seriously diminished without it and considerably enhanced by it. The very nature of a game suggests the need for a discussion during which the various activities that occurred simultaneously during play, and were thus obscured to many players, can be brought together to describe a total picture.

While students can benefit from playing a game among themselves, as a kind of interlude or diversion from ordinary classroom activities, an important opportunity would be wasted if the teacher simply returned to conventional activities without discussing it.

Discussion Points

In debriefing a game, the teacher can begin discussion with concrete and unthreatening kinds of questions. Students have just participated in an activity. They know what they did. They probably know why. They know who won or did not win. There is little reluctance to describe the situation. Typically, the postgame discussion begins with the determination of winners, or the scoring. The winning individual or team ought to be asked what actions they took in the game and why they thought these helped them to win. Similarly, individuals or teams that did not win can be asked to describe what they did, how they decided to take the actions they chose, and why these were less successful than those of the winning team.

How much the game seemed to depend on chance factors, or how much control students felt they had over the success of their actions, should be discussed. Whether or not students felt the game was fair (sometimes games are weighted against a particular team) may reveal something about the process explored. In the game of Colony, one team plays the British government in the eighteenth century. This team is doomed to expend more money to administrate the American colonies than they can take in from taxes on colonial trade. Initially, the British government players do not know that the game is stacked against them. In discovering this in the course of the game, students will learn some of the problems the British government faced during that period.

In games that require negotiation, the interactions among players should be analyzed. Who spoke to whom? How did they try to persuade other players to their view? If successful, why do they think they succeeded in changing another player's mind? Why did that player ally with others? What did he think was the most convincing argument? (Interesting differences in perception may arise here.) Why were some players limited to negotiating with only a few others? In the game of Section, for example, conservative farmers who do not want any state money expended in their section for fear of increasing the government's power are not allowed to seek interaction with players outside their section. They may talk to anyone who approaches them but in reality they would be unlikely to campaign for their views outside their own section. Similarly, unemployed workers cannot move outside their section because they would have little access to more substantial citizens and they probably could not afford to move around the state. A more significant constraint on interaction is implicit in the governmental structure of the game. Citizens of any one section talk only to their political representatives, rather than to those of other sections, or to the executive committee superimposed on the legislature.

Through discussion of concrete facts about the playing of the game, students will reveal much about the process involved. The teacher can then lead the class to a discussion of the process, relying less on specific facts about game play but using these facts where it helps to illustrate a point. After playing Section, for example, students can discuss such points as the problem of limited resources, the need for compromise produced by limited resources, the nature of political sanctions in making one's interests and influence felt, the nature of interest groups, the problems political representatives face in attempting to reconcile conflicting interests.

Similarly, a discussion of Colony might cover the need for any government in any period to gain revenue to support its own functions, the particular method of doing this in the eighteenth century British Empire, the conflict between the interests of the British government and the interest of colonial traders, the difficulty of enforcing law in the face of opposition and evasion.

In the simulation of the Continental Congresses, the peaceful attempts of the colonists to obtain legal redress of their grievances, the frustration of those attempts, the impact of "accidental" events (Lexington and Concord), the objectivity of reporting those events, the cautious development of opinion in favor of independence, the division of opinion ranging from "radical" to "conservative," the uncertainty of success once independence is declared, or the different course of action that players took when compared to the actions of the real colonists should be fruitful points for discussion.

But there is yet another step before the game can be considered exploited to full advantage.

Integrating Games into the Curriculum

It is unlikely that games that have been thoroughly debriefed will be subsequently ignored. That would be most unfortunate. Students are quick to pick up the implication that an activity "doesn't count" and rapidly learn the sequence or boundaries of the activity the teacher considers peripheral. One could imagine students becoming accustomed to the "briefing, play, debriefing" routine and then returning to "serious" material. Not that the experience of the game is likely to be erased. But the teacher can guarantee that students will exploit that experience when pursuing the subject area in other media. This function of integration of all curriculum materials is a critical one.

Again, examples may serve to demonstrate how the teacher can integrate games with other materials. Section is used in a unit on political geography. By referring to the game, various study topics such as the definition of territory, the relationship between the natural resources and economics of a section to its political interests, the conflict of interests produced in part by natural differences in resources, and topography can be made more concrete, and hence more comprehensible.

In the historical trade game, several issues that later became major sources of conflict between Britain and the American colonies are presented. Traders have the opportunity to smuggle goods into the colonies and thus evade paying customs duties. Britain has the opportunity to substitute British judges for colonial juries in trials of smugglers who are caught. In discussing the Revolution and evaluating the claims of the protagonists, students who have played the game will be able to compare the colonists' claim of burdensome taxes to their own ability to pay taxes in the game. Take the question of "British tyranny" in eliminating colonial juries; this could be discussed in terms of players' experience in the game, where colonial juries frequently failed to convict traders who were obviously guilty of smuggling. In analyzing causes of the American Revolution, students should be able to go beyond the simplified explanations that the British taxed heavily—a point contradicted by players' experience in the game.

By referring to the student's direct and concrete experience in a game, the teacher can make the game both academically and psychologically important and in so doing, enhance the importance of all materials. School time is too precious to waste. There's no room for "peripheral" activities.

The Teacher's Role: A Reprise

In debriefing a game, the teacher assumes a more dominant role than he played in the game. Does this imply that the game is simply an interlude for the teacher during which he temporarily takes a back seat? The author thinks not. While the debriefing relies heavily on the teacher's leadership, the nature of the discussion is largely determined by the fact that it is focused on a game. There is still no right or wrong answer. Students are involved in analyzing their own actions and discovering the rationalizations of their peers. While the teacher may have returned to the front of the classroom, he is helping his students to evaluate their own actions and performance, rather than handing down judgments from above. In fact, he is still functioning as coach. If the title sounds mundane, it should not be forgotten that the coach usually makes the team. The teacher still makes education.

CHAPTER 5

DESIGN AND ADAPTATION OF GAMES

5

Tracing a Game Design

Designing Games in Class

Game Adaptability

Designing games can be an extremely difficult, frustrating activity. But like most creative efforts, it is highly rewarding. For the teacher, game design can not only produce useful, effective classroom exercises, but can be personally instructive. Even more exciting is the possibility of encouraging classes to design their own games, for the analysis and decision making necessary to creating a game is probably more educational than participation in a fully designed game.

This chapter is devoted to outlining the process of game design: first, by tracing the development of a finished game; second, by describing the steps that teachers might follow in developing a game idea, either among themselves or with their classes. It should be emphasized that retracing the development of a finished game through ten basic steps is far easier than using those ten steps as a recipe for the development of a new game. Game design is not a science. It is closer to being art, for the basic guidelines or rules for design tend to be useful only to a point. While all the ten steps must be considered in the course of designing the game, they do not necessarily fall into a sequential order. They do represent, however, a useful starting point and a checklist in a process where inspiration is an important, if unwritten, requirement.

To begin, it would probably be best for a group of teachers to develop a simple game for use in the classroom. With this experience, teachers could then work with their students in designing a game that describes or simulates a process the class is studying.

Since producing a completed game is a time-consuming process, not all of the development could take place in class. Research is often required, or written materials must be produced, and these tasks could be done by students as homework. It would not be rash to suggest that this homework would be most palatable. First, the class as a whole depends on each member to contribute his share, else the entire process might be delayed or disrupted. For the student, this is a potent incentive to be responsible. Second, the activity itself, while it is educational, has immediate practical application in the classroom, for whatever the student has discovered or produced will be integrated into the game. Further, the quality of that contribution will be evaluated by the game itself or by the student's peers. No single authority needs to judge the effort. And if a student's contribution to the game does not work in practice, the aim of creating a game will usually dominate over temporary disappointment. For students, the importance of contributing to an exercise that will be *used* cannot be overemphasized. The value of creating a *product* cannot be overestimated. Not all learning must be directed toward practical goals. But probably the major deficiency of the schools today is their failure to convince students that their years in school are related to their postschool lives. Directing students in activities that treat real-world issues in real-world ways is a step toward reducing alienation.

Tracing a Game Design

The game of Manchester was designed for use with a high school history unit on the Industrial Revolution in England. The game focuses on the migration of laborers from country to city, which was partly induced by the development of industry and which in turn was a critical factor in making possible the further development of industry. The following is a step-by-step retracing of the design process for Manchester.

Game Purpose

Step 1. Define design objectives. In designing any game, its purpose should first be established. This may range from education to analysis to diagnostic testing. The general purpose of Manchester is education. This, of course, would be the primary purpose of any games that students would help to design.

More specifically, the basic purpose of Manchester is to teach students some of the economic pressures and social interactions that operated in the historical process of industrialization.

Scope

Step 2. Determine the scope of the game in terms of the issues to be examined, its setting in time, and its geographic area. In effect, this step represents defining the subject of the game. Since Manchester was developed as part of a curriculum unit on the Industrial Revolution in England, the specific place and period were already determined. But even if the game were designed independent of any curriculum unit, the early stages in the first country to industrialize would be the best choice for examining the process in the simplest way. It is not essential that players know the precise period and place—England in the late eighteenth century—to be able to participate.

The basic issue of the game is the impact that parallel developments in agriculture and industry made on the laboring population and, in turn, the impact of the changing urban and rural patterns on each other. More specifically, farmers who could consolidate their land holdings could produce more with fewer laborers. This made it more difficult for laborers to obtain employment in the countryside or to maintain wage levels. As a parallel, small-scale industry in the city could grow only if laborers could be attracted. Wage levels in the city were typically higher, therefore, than in the countryside and this induced many workers to leave the farms.

To emphasize the relations between the rural and urban economies, Manchester is set at a time when some industry already existed. The game focuses on the push-pull hypothesis of the rural-to-urban migration, examining those factors that pushed laborers off the farms and attracted them to the cities. The precise analysis is a chicken-or-egg question; historians tend to emphasize either the attraction of the city or the changes in agriculture as decisive in producing the enormous flow of population to industries and cities. The two factors operate simultaneously in Manchester, probably the fairest assessment of the historical process.

A deliberate decision was made not to set the game at a time prior to the existence of industry. To have gamed industrialization from its earliest identifiable point would have required emphasis on technological advances, an extremely complicated problem. This could have been done to some extent by introducing new technologies in menu or chance-card form, permitting players to utilize machines if they could raise the capital to acquire them. This would probably have complicated and lengthened the game unnecessarily in terms of the designers' objectives.

Defining the scope of a game looks deceptively easy. It is often difficult to decide, particularly in historical games, at what point in a process the game should begin. In a simulation of the Continental Congress, for example, the designers faced the problem of whether to begin at the first session or at some later point. Any alternative required some simplifications and minor distortions. In the end, the simulation did start at the first meeting of the Congress but ignored the problem of perfect historical accuracy with regard to delegates who did not attend or arrive until later sessions.

Key Actors

Step 3. Identify key actors in the process, whether individuals, groups, organizations, or institutions. This is a fairly easy step. In Manchester, the key actors are laborers, mill owners, farmers, and a squire or major landowner. Actors are defined by function, which means that an actor could represent a group rather than an individual.

The designers must also decide how many players are necessary or desirable. In Manchester, the number of players is seven or nine; seven seemed the minimum number necessary for acting out the process. There are two mill owners, two farmers, one squire who owns most of the land, and either two or four laborers. These later actors actually represent families of workers, and must find employment for a total of sixteen laborers (eight or four each, depending on the number of players). The reason for selecting this number was to guarantee that a surplus population would be available for employment as industry expands. In addition, laborers are pressured into accepting fairly low wages, as the labor supply in the game usually exceeds the demand.

Sometimes, the number of players is predetermined and the game must be developed to satisfy that situation. For example, it is often desirable to have the class as a whole participate in one game. This simplifies the teacher's job of supervising, as it is easier to administer one game for thirty players than two simultaneous games for fifteen players each. Sometimes this necessity suggests having a team, rather than an individual, play a function or role. For example, in Manchester, each mill owner, farmer, and so on could be played by a team of two or three students. Or, instead of having a few players represent many laborers, each of the sixteen required could be a live player. There are some disadvantages to the solution since increasing the number of laborers would lengthen negotiation cycles.

While there is a great deal of flexibility in deciding the number of players, some attention should be paid to the actual ratios. The number of laborers did in fact exceed the number of entrepreneurs, and this is accounted for in Manchester.

Another point to remember is the frequent need for assigning players to housekeeping functions. Particularly in games for big groups, simple money transactions, for example, become time-consuming because of the large number of players. In Manchester, it is suggested that the squire perform the banking function since his role is somewhat less active than the others. This doubling up is feasible in many games. However, in games where each actor is continually active, one or two students should be asked to act exclusively as bankers. Although these students do learn from the game, the number of housekeeping roles should be kept to a minimum.

Player Goals

Step 4. Define the objectives of the actors, in terms of wealth, power, influence, and other rewards. Actors in a game must know what goals they are trying to achieve. In the game of Manchester, each actor has the overall objective of increasing his wealth as much as possible. This is, of course, a simplification. Men are not motivated by monetary factors alone. The game is, however, about an economic process where the desire to increase wealth was a potent influence on men's behavior. It also focuses attention on the disparity of wealth between increasingly rich entrepreneurs and terribly poor laborers. In addition, the medium of money is a convenient game device, a point that should not be overlooked.

Specific objectives must also be defined in terms of the *means* or context of increasing wealth. For each actor in Manchester there is a different type of economic activity. Mill owners produce cloth and must expand production to increase profits. Farmers produce wheat and must expand their land holdings and their production to increase profit. Laborers must find employment either on the farms or in the mills to earn wages. If they do not find employment they are permitted to weave cloth in cottage industry for a fixed return that is lower than their subsistence requirements.

Defining the objectives of actors in a game is particularly difficult when those objectives are not material. Ideological objectives, such as maintaining a particular political position, are often difficult to make operational. Simply stating the player's political position for him does not guarantee he will be motivated to argue it during the course of play. In games where political debate has direct impact on an economic cycle for example, the player can perceive the relationship and argue the position which is to his advantage. In pure simulations, where the entire exercise consists of debate, the problem is also less serious. However, in many of the hybrid games, it is important to tie any ideological viewpoints to ways of acting on them. For example, in a game about Reconstruction after the Civil War, radical congressmen who want to reform the South must be given channels for doing so (such as persuading Congress to approve a plan to confiscate plantation land and redistribute it to ex-slaves and poor white farmers). Simply asking players to argue a position, without providing a means for implementing it, is unlikely to provide the players with sufficient impetus.

Player Resources

Step 5. Determine the actors' resources, including the game information each receives. Player resources may range from very tangible assets, such as money, to intangible advantages, such as social status. In Manchester, all actors have economic resources in the form of money. In addition, the squire owns land and the mill owners start with one machine each. Farmers own one plot of land and are assumed to have a long-term lease, from the squire, on two other plots.

What is more difficult is determining precisely how much money, land, or other resources each player should begin with. The first decision to make is whether or not each player within an actor category should receive the same or different amounts. It is desirable to minimize differences within a group to avoid the complication of distributing different amounts of money to each individual. In Manchester, farmers all start with the same amount of money and land. Mill owners are similarly undifferentiated, as are laborers. Sometimes, however, it is desirable to demonstrate the effects of different initial resources within the same actor group. Where chances for success or behavior heavily depend on the resources a player starts with, the distinctions should be made.

Once the question of uniformity or diversity is resolved, the hard work of assigning quantities must be done. There is usually no formula for calculating the proper ratios. Unfortunately, the process of assigning quantities is often one of trial and error. But amounts can be extremely important in influencing the behavior of players in the game. In one test of a game about geographic expansion, players were given too much money to start with. As a result, the process of developing many small farms was distorted because players were able to accumulate far more land than the real historical actors could. The players' initial resources had to be adjusted to make it more difficult for them to acquire large amounts of land. Insuring that the quantities assigned in the game facilitate play and do not distort the process simply requires patience. There is no need, though, to attempt to use figures closely corresponding to the real situation. In Manchester, the resources of different actors indicate their different positions without actually representing the historical ratios.

Another important resource in any game is the information each actor requires to be able to play. In simulations, the players usually need role profiles defining their positions on the issues involved, and describing the circumstances, if any, under which they would modify their stands. In some games, special information is given to some players and withheld from others. For example, in a game about revolution, the government is not told who the revolutionaries are. For the revolutionaries, anonymity is a powerful resource.

In Manchester, players need basically simple items of information to function in the game. These data are so closely related to the decisions they must make that the information requirements are best determined and described at the time the decision rules are set up.

Decision Rules

Step 6. Determine the decision rules, or criteria, that actors use in deciding what actions to take. The basic decisions that the various actors must make constitute the foundation of the game. In Manchester, mill owners and farmers must make production decisions as a means to increasing their wealth. Mill owners may buy machines and hire labor to work them. Farmers may lease or buy land from the squire and hire labor to work it.

These decisions require information about the price of land, the price of machines, and the number of laborers required to work either land or machines. In addition, these actors need to know what output to expect from large machines or additional (and particularly consolidated or adjacent) landholdings. Such information is presented to mill owners in the form of a cloth production schedule, while farmers get a wheat production schedule. From the production schedules, players can see that they may benefit from economies of scale. For example, two cloth machines, each worked by one man, yield forty bolts of cloth; but one two-man machine will yield fifty bolts of cloth. Similarly, one plot worked by the farmer who owns it yields ten bushels of wheat; but two adjacent plots could be worked by the one farmer, and this arrangement yields twenty-four bushels of wheat.

The production schedules are not really complicated to develop, especially if the designer has some knowledge of economics. Information about the price of wheat and cloth is deliberately withheld. Mill owners and farmers must make their production decisions under conditions of uncertainty about what to expect in return. They are, however, given an average price for guidance.

Once mill owners and farmers have decided whether to purchase additional machinery or land, they must decide how much they wish to spend on labor and then go about hiring laborers. This action is not independent, since the laborers are actual players who must be bargained with.

The laborer must decide where to work (country or city) and for what wages. What opportunities exist will depend on the prior actions of the landowners or farmers, which determine how many jobs are available. Assuming that mill owners and farmers do not increase the number of machines and land plots they own, only four jobs are available in the city. Likewise, only four jobs exist in the countryside (each farmer starts with three plots, and works one himself). Since there are sixteen labor tokens in the game, there are fewer available jobs than workers. To offset this deliberate disparity, the designers built in another option for the laborers: they may work in the countryside in cottage industry, producing cloth at a fixed return. Once laborers (all but two of whom begin in the country) decide where they will seek work, they must decide what minimum wages to accept. Farmers and mill owners would wish to pay as little as possible. However, laborers (and all other players) are given a subsistence requirement, and they must earn enough to pay the cost. (Each actor's subsistence cost varies according to his position.) To motivate players to seek employment either on the farms or in the mills, the fixed return they receive from cottage industry is lower than the cost of subsistence they must pay.

The squire has relatively few decisions to make. He may rent or lease his land on any terms he and the farmer agree on. In addition, mill owners are given the option of borrowing money from the squire (the richest player) to enable them to expand even without sufficient cash in hand.

Player Interaction

Step 7. Determine the interaction sequence among the actors. The pattern of interaction in Manchester is as follows:

Mill owners need labor	Laborers need work
Farmers need labor	Laborers need work
Mill owners need machines	(Bank)
Mill owners need money for machines	Squire has money
Farmers need more land	Squire owns land

Only one interaction is unnecessary: the squire and laborers need not communicate with each other. Farmers and mill owners need not communicate unless the farmer loses his money and land, in which case he may become a laborer and seek work in the city.

Constraints

Step 8. Identify external constraints on the actions of the actors. In any game, it is necessary to define not only what

the actors may and should do, but what they may not do. Not
every possible option needs to be considered and identified
as allowed or disallowed. It is nearly impossible to account
for every alternative. However, there are natural constraints
on the actions of real-world actors that should be incorporated into the game. For example, in a game where Quakers
are actors, violence should be disallowed for that group.
In Manchester, several constraints are imposed. First, since
collective bargaining by laborers was prohibited at the time,
this action is prohibited in the game; attempts to bargain
collectively are penalized by a fine of £ 1. This constraint
represents the Combination Acts in England, which made
collective action illegal.

To point up class differences, and to avoid complicating
the game unduly, the squire is not permitted to work land
himself. This ensures that he must live off his rents and mo-
tivates him to rent to farmers. In addition, he is not permitted
to move to the city or establish a mill. For a landed gentle-
man, this would have been considered undesirable, even if
the financial gains were attractive. In game terms, it insures
that the operation of the countryside is not unrealistically
distorted.

Scoring

Step 9. Decide the scoring rules or win criteria of the game.
Scoring should be defined in terms of the objectives of the
actors. The degree to which actors achieve the objectives
established for them is a measurement of who wins. In the
case of Manchester, scoring is fairly simple since the objectives are stated uniformly in terms of money. To be per-
fectly accurate, however, the winner is not simply the player
with the most money at the end but the player with the most
money once each player divides his total sum by his initial
resources.

This decision is a more difficult one in the case of games
where different actors have different objectives. In a game
on the Reconstruction, for example, all players wish to
increase their wealth; but ex-slaves also seek education.
Where there is diversity in objectives, some convenient
conversion method is required so that education might be
translated into a sum of money, or (more palatably) that
money, education, and other goals are all translated into a
point system.

This step is often extremely difficult to decide before the
very end of the design process. But it should be considered
all along the way, because it helps alert the designers to items
that have no function in the game.

Presentation and Rules

Step 10. Choose form of presentation (board game, role playing) and formulate sequence of operations. The choice between a role-play game and a board game is a fairly obvious one. Where discussion of issues based on written profiles is the substance of the game, a board is unnecessary. Where a process is described, some form of gameboard to record or focus the action is useful. Board games are somewhat more difficult to design well because the board should be an integral part of the game, not just a colorful gimmick. If the game requires the use of land, for example, a board is a good way to record who owns land and how it is used. There is no need for one large board used in common by all players; individual farms, for instance, could just as well be separate, small boards. In games for a whole class, it is particularly difficult to fit all players around a single board. Several medium-sized boards spaced around the room have another advantage over one enormous board: They encourage movement, which supports the relatively free atmosphere of games.

Manchester uses one board. The village is represented at one end, and the squire and farmers sit here. Mill owners sit at the other end, where the city and its mills are represented. Laborers sit between the two groups, opposite a road connecting city and country. The board serves several important functions. Landowners can identify their land in the village by placing blocks on top of the squares. Mill owners place tokens representing machines on their end of the board. These tokens (dominoes have been used consistently) show how many laborers are needed. Since the laborers' tokens are also kept on the board, and are placed on either land or machines when workers are hired, students can get a fairly good picture of the supply and demand situation and calculate accordingly.

The *sequence of operations* that the designers must determine essentially represents the rules of the game. It usually is the last step in game design, summarizing the designers' previous analysis in a form that can be used by the players. It is advisable, however, to attempt to fill out the sequence of action throughout the course of design. In writing up the sequence, the designers often discover omissions and ambiguities, which can be resolved at that time. Also, any major periods of inactivity for some players can be noted and reduced.

The Game of Manchester: A Recap

The sequence of activities that was finally outlined for Manchester is as follows:

1. Mill owners buy textile machinery from the bank. They may borrow money from the squire to do so. At the same time, farmers lease or buy land from the squire.

During this initial step (which in the early phases of the game is likely to be very brief because expansion is more likely to occur later), laborers have no specific activity. However, this is not serious because the decisions of the other actors have direct bearing on what the laborers' bargaining position will be. If farmers or mill owners expand a great deal, the demand for labor is increased and some laborers will begin to see the advantage themselves.

2. Laborers decide whether to move more tokens to the city or to keep three of their four tokens in the countryside. This decision may not be changed during a cycle of play. To limit movement between city and country, and to encourage players to think about their decision, a transportation fee (£ 1) is charged whenever a token is moved.

3. Mill owners and farmers then negotiate with laborers for their services. Laborers may have distributed their tokens in the city and the country, in which case they negotiate with both mill owners and farmers. They may accept different wages for any labor token; that is, each laborer does not necessarily negotiate for all of his tokens as a bloc.

When laborers are hired, tokens representing them are placed on the appropriate machine or land plot.

Any laborers who remain unemployed in the country are placed on a space on the board representing cottage industry. Any laborers who remain unemployed in the city have no alternative means of earning money.

During this negotiation, any attempt at collective bargaining should be penalized by a fine of £1 on each laborer. This should be determined either by the teacher or the squire.

4. The next step is to determine the output of the farms and mills based on the arrangement of land plots and size of machines, and whether or not there is labor to work them. The number of bushels of wheat and bolts of cloth is determined by looking at the production schedules.

5. Next, laborers and mill owners must find out how much money they will receive from the bank for each bushel of wheat and each bolt of cloth they have produced. This information is presented in the form of chance cards. Cloth and wheat price cards may be turned up by players assigned to do so. After the total sum due the farmers and mill owners has been calculated, these players collect their money from the bank.

Steps 4 and 5 do not take too much time so the laborers

are not inactive for long. The seriousness of this lag had to be determined in test plays.

6. Accounts are then settled. Farmers pay rent to the squire. Mill owners and farmers pay wages to the laborers, according to their previous agreement.

7. Subsistence costs are then paid to the bank. The amount each player owes should be presented to the players in their rules or in chart form. Each laborer pays a subsistence cost for *each* labor token he manipulates.

Here, a question arises as to what happens to a player who cannot pay subsistence. In the case of the squire and mill owners, this is unlikely to happen. Farmers probably will not face this problem but if they do, they may sell their land back to the bank, using that money to pay rent or subsistence. They can then farm the land that remains or, if completely ruined, seek work as a laborer.

For the laborers, this is a fairly likely situation. For that reason, a workhouse (or poorhouse) was built into the game, simulating the historical Poor Laws. Any player, including any individual tokens of the laborers, who cannot pay subsistence is placed in the workhouse for the next cycle of play. That player or token cannot make any bargains or transact any business while there. Players do not have to pay subsistence cost while in the workhouse and may choose to stay there longer than necessary but, in that case, they cannot participate in the game. To discourage players from accepting the workhouse as a comfortable alternative to working for less than subsistence, each time the same worker is committed to the workhouse his stay is increased. For example, the third time a worker goes to the workhouse, he must stay for three cycles.

The squire and mill owners operate the workhouse. Workers may be hired at a fixed wage. This money goes to the bank to cover the cost of operating the workhouse (a fixed sum per occupant). However, any deficit in the workhouse's budget must be made up by equal payments to the bank from the squire and mill owners. Transaction of workhouse business is the last step in the cycle. The entire sequence then repeats.

While Manchester is fairly easy to play and administer, it is a complex game based on a complex process and required a fair amount of research to develop. In addition, the skills of economists facilitated the development process.

Games requiring less research and less specialized knowledge are, of course, easier and quicker to design. A game like Manchester requires one designer approximately three months to develop. A simpler game sould probably be developed by a teacher and his students in one month of classroom time, providing various components of the game were developed by students outside of class and the teacher put in his normal amount of preparation time. A very simple game, such as a job interview simulation, could be done in a maximum of two weeks class time, including play.

Designing Games in Class

Before attempting to have students design a game, the teacher should first choose a topic under study that could be translated usefully into game form. This step is extremely important, and a few basic guidelines are suggested.

First, *select a process*. Games are most useful for presenting dynamic processes, where many aspects of a problem can be treated simultaneously. It is this characteristic that makes it so difficult to design a game, retrace a game design, or describe a game in prose or in the form of rules. The nature of description is sequential (one thing at a time) while the nature of a game is dynamic (many things at once).

Second, *avoid attempting to convey a list of facts in game form*. It is not worth spending the design time or playing time on a game whose only purpose is to convey facts. There are more efficient means (the textbook is a notable one) of accomplishing that end. The teacher should test a proposed game problem by asking: Is the problem dynamic? Is it important? Can it be taught as easily in text or other form? Are there intangible elements of the problem that are not effectively conveyed in text?

In essence, selecting the game topic and defining the objectives of the game—or what the students should learn from playing it (step 1 of game design)—are the same thing. The objectives should be stated as specifically as possible. "To teach about the Industrial Revolution," for example, is too vague a statement of purpose. "To teach that industry developed partly because it was able to attract labor away from the farms" is somewhat better. The more specific the designer can be in defining the process, the better the game and the easier the design procedure. For example, the following would be a concrete statement of objectives and a good beginning in game design: "To teach that as technological advances made large-scale production possible, entrepreneurs invested capital and sought labor to operate machines; that a laboring population was available which could be attracted by higher wages than were paid in agriculture; that at the same time, agriculture was undergoing changes which created a surplus laboring population, available for factory work."

This quickly leads into the question of scope. If the problem selected is too general, or spans too long a time, it will be extremely difficult, or impossible, to game it in an accurate way.

Another type of issue that is difficult to game is a purely ideological one. If the teacher's purpose is to teach two different ideologies, he can probably do it best in written form. However, if the teacher wants to show the impact of two different ideologies on the organization of society, that would be possible and useful to game. One question that should be asked in selecting a game problem is "What do the players have to decide?" If this question cannot be answered because the players are simply asked to recite a given position, the result will be a recitation, not a game. On the other hand, if players are asked to decide such matters as who in the community will vote, who will pay taxes, and who will work, a game using ideological positions in deciding issues can be developed.

Once a topic has been selected, the teacher can present the issue to the class and organize the design procedure. Since design is really *not* a step-by-step process, it is suggested that the ten major points to be decided be listed on the board. As the broad outlines of the game are defined, more and more details can be filled in as questions arise. For example, when step 4 (actors' objectives) has been determined, attention might naturally turn to step 9 (win criteria). As the actors' resources (step 5) are filled in, parts of step 7 (the interaction sequence among the actors) might be decided in parallel.

What follows is the author's attempt to show the actual, spontaneous procedure a designer might use in the initial development of a game. A role-play game has been chosen deliberately, partly because it requires less mathematical calculation, and partly to provide contrast with Manchester. Besides, it offers clearly defined tasks that students can do as individual homework assignments, thereby reducing the amount of classroom time necessary to develop the game.

Let us take, for example, a game about labor-management relations and the process of collective bargaining. The following chart represents the first stage in the design of a game called Strike.

Game of Strike — Work Sheet 1

1. Objectives

The objective of the game of Strike is to teach students:
1. The costs and benefits to labor of collective action
2. The costs of strikes to management (and possibly to the public)
3. The nature of compromise
4. The role of government (this might be optional)

2. Scope

The game might begin on the eve of the expiration of a contract. Labor and management might negotiate to draw up a new contract within x days or a strike is threatened. Alternatively, the game might begin on the first day of a strike to avoid possibility of settlement prior to the strike.

3. Actors

1. Laborers — rank and file, and a few leaders
2. Management of industry
3. State or federal government

4. Actors' Objectives

1. Laborers want increased wages. (To avoid complication, wages might be the only issue.)
2. Management wants to pay as little as possible, but also seeks to avoid or end (depending on when game starts) a strike.
3. Government wants to avoid taking action if possible; also wants to prevent disruption of public life or shortage of an important product (depending on industry selected).

5. Resources

1. Labor — withholds services; union has reserve funds.
2. Management — money to hold out.
3. Government — has legal power to intervene and effect settlement (too early in plans to be more specific).

6. Decision Rules

Both labor and management must decide when to agree to a settlement.

This depends in part on the resources each has for prolonging negotiation. Government must decide whether and when to intervene. Labor and management teams will need to be cued as to what (minimum) (maximum) settlement will be. Government will need to be cued on when to intervene. This might be x number of days.

7. Interaction Sequence — Basic interaction is negotiation between the two labor and management teams.

8. Constraints — No union member may make an individual settlement. Management may not attempt to settle with individual workers. (It would be unrealistic to allow such actions.)

9. Scoring Rules — This depends on specific statement of actors' objectives. A point scale might be used to determine which team (labor or management) came closest to securing objective of gaining $x per week increase or paying no more than $x per week.

10. Sequence of Action — This should permit alternation of two basic sessions:
1. Secret strategy sessions for labor and management
2. Negotiations sessions between labor and management

At this point a rough outline of the game has been made. This was a fairly easy, nonstop, unpremeditated process for the author. Many specific decisions that will constitute the details of the game have been postponed for the sake of filling out a broad picture. Now it is time to make those decisions. One possible source of difficulty is the government. There may not be enough for a live government team to do. To avoid building in boring roles, it might be better to substitute a set of government cards for real players.

The crude game outline now existing is probably sufficient to present to the class. Students may now be involved in contributing to the design. The following worksheets illustrate successive stages in the development of the game.

Game of Strike — Work Sheet 2

1. Objectives   Same

2. Scope   Perhaps the best compromise here is to begin the game on the last day before the contract expires and the strike begins. Each cycle of the game might represent one day and could last fifteen minutes in class. Thus it would be unlikely for students to settle in the first round. The game ends when the two teams agree. (The end of a game is not always so obvious. Often, an arbitrary number of class periods or rounds must be set as the limit.)

3. Actors   Let's leave government "in the cards." Number of players is the next question. Two teams of fifteen each is probably unwieldy — might limit active participation of maximum number of students. Teams of five each would probably be best but this might leave teacher with three simultaneous games to supervise. Compromise at two sets of two teams of approximately seven players each. Labor team should be two leaders, five rank and file. Management team: president, treasurer, and five other undifferentiated management players.

4. Actors' Objectives   Too early to be more specific

5. Resources   Labor:
1. Each laborer must be given a wage level. For now, let us say each laborer makes $100 per week.
2. Union has fund to pay members half salary for x weeks. (For uniformity, this may have to be translated into days, instead of weeks.)
Management:
1. Can lose $x without hurting end-of-year profit. This amount is in terms of *not* taking in $x profit per day so that team is pressured to settle within a certain number of days.

6. Decision Rules

Information on when company will suffer and when union funds run out is key influence on decision to settle. However, competing influence is long-term extrapolation of what a particular settlement will cost for the year. Similarly for labor—holding out for best settlement may take so long as to hurt total income for year.

7. Interaction Sequence

Same

8. Constraints

Consider requiring labor to pay subsistence costs. Careful—this may complicate game too much.

9. Scoring Rules

10. Sequence of Action

Game of Strike — Work Sheet 3

1. Objective

Same

2. Scope

Have the class select an actual industry or make up a hypothetical one.

A hypothetical industry would be simpler for the purpose of focusing on the negotiation process; an actual industry would be better if the characteristics of a particular industry are a teaching objective. Probably easier to do basic process and fill in details of an industry later. Assign one or two students to write a scenario describing the situation: Negotiations look unpromising; strike imminent; issue is wages. This ought to be in journalistic style and suggest sympathies of community. Only information available to both teams should be included.

3. Actors

Information on objectives should be presented in form of profiles. Only two profiles are needed, one for each team. These might give some background of hypothetical company and of hypothetical union to generate team identification.

4. Actors' Objectives

Let's try this:
Laborers make $20 per day or $100 per week or $5200 per year.
Laborers want $25 per day or $125 per week or $6500 per year.
Question remains: Should this be minimum they want and below which they will not settle, or ideal solution but will agree to less?

5. Resources

Laborers receive pay for only one day from union. (This is neater than half pay for two days.)

6. Decision Rules

Then, for every day out of work they lose $20 (a record of this should be kept). This means that if strike lasts one (simulated) month or twenty working days, laborers lose $400. Since this is relatively small amount compared to potential $1300 annual increase (still leaving $900 net gain), the above figure ($25 per day or $1300 annual increase) should probably be maximum. Minimum satisfactory settlement for laborers might be $22 per day or $110 per week or $5720 per year, for an increase of $520. This would mean labor would gain nothing for the year if the strike lasted twenty-seven days. ($20 \times 26 = 520$ plus 1 day paid by union.)

7. Interaction Sequence

8. Constraints

Subsistence costs for labor now appear unnecessary. It is the strategy for overall gain that is important and motivating. "Daily expenses" need not be built in.

9. Scoring Rules

10. Sequence of Action

Game of Strike—Work Sheet 4

1. Objectives

2. Scope

3. Actors

4. Actors' Objectives   Objective of Management is to limit wages to a maximum of $5330 per year or $130 increase per year per worker.

5. Resources   Management: Pays $5200 to each laborer per year. Wishes to pay $5330 per year without raising prices or reducing profit ($20.50 per day or $102.50 per week).
See Step 4 above.

6. Decision Rules   Management team needs further detail on resources, costs, and benefits.

7. Interaction Sequence

8. Constraints

9. Scoring Rules

10. Sequence of Action

Game of Strike — Work Sheet 5

1. Objectives

2. Scope

3. Actors

4. Actors' Objectives

Current outlines suggests problem of too quick resolution and perhaps not enough competitive pressure on teams to trade off different objectives. Thus should add at least one other category of conflict — vacation time. Laborers' objectives become, in order of priority:
1. Increased wages
2. Longer vacation
Note: Students might research the kinds of benefits labor seeks. But try to limit number of benefits in the game for sake of simplicity.

5. Resources

6. Decision Rules

7. Interaction Sequence

8. Constraints

9. Scoring Rules

10. Sequence of Action

Game of Strike—Worksheet 6

1. Objectives

2. Scope

3. Actors

4. Actors' Objectives   Management priorities: Will increase wages to $5330 and vacation time by 1 week.
Labor: Will hold out for higher wages and sacrifice vacation time.

5. Resources   Management: $5500 maximum to spend per laborer.

6. Decision   Costs to management: Wage increase and extra week's vacation ($100 per laborer) is O.K. if under $5500. For each day of strike after first 5 days, company loses $10 per day per worker.

7. Interaction Sequence

8. Constraints

9. Scoring Rules

10. Sequence of Action   Negotiation need only occur on basis of wages of one laborer. For the sake of simplicity, no calculations of overall company finances are presented.

Game of Strike — Worksheet 7

1. Objectives

2. Scope

For simplicity, ignore government role. Once game is built and tried, government cards might be introduced after x rounds. Or teacher might play role of government, thereby giving the teacher the opportunity to control game from within.

3. Actors

4. Actors' Objectives

5. Resources

6. Decision Rules

Information on wage increase should be presented in chart form. One student or a few could put this together:

	Yearly	Daily
Current Wage	$5200	$20.00
	5330	20.50 = Company maximum
	5460	21.00
	5590	21.50
	5720	22.00 = Labor minimum
	5850	22.50
	5980	23.00
	6110	23.50
	6240	24.00
	6370	24.50
	6500	25.00

7. Interaction Sequence

8. Constraints

9. Scoring Rules

Winner is team that comes closest to objective on above possible wage scale. To calculate this, labor must subtract from agreed wage level any loss from prolonged strike. Management must add to agreed wage level any loss from strike. Both add $100 to wage scale if vacation time is increased.

10. Sequence of Action

The Game of Strike — Summary

The game begins on the day before the contract between
Union X and Company Y expires.

Players. Seven laborers who are union members (one is president of the union, and one is treasurer) and seven company
representatives (one is president of the company, and one is
treasurer).

Resources. The union has enough money to pay wages to its
members for one day of the strike. After that, players receive
no pay.
   The company can survive five days of a strike without losing
money. After that, the company loses $10 per day for each
laborer (calculations are made for only one laborer, however).

Objectives. The objectives of labor (the union) are to achieve
a pay increase to $5720 and an additional week's vacation.
   The objective of management is to pay as little as possible
and avoid an additional week's vacation. The company does
not wish to pay more than $5500 per year per laborer.
   (The specific financial information should be given only to
the team to which it applies.)

Action. The action of the game consists of two alternating
cycles of approximately fifteen minutes each.
   1. The union meets to plan strategy for the bargaining
      session. It may ask for increases far above what it will
      actually settle for.
   At the same time, in another part of the room management
meets to plan strategy. It may likewise offer nothing, or less
than they are willing to settle for.
   2. When the strategy session is over, the two teams face
      each other. The union presents its demand. The company
      accepts or makes a counteroffer. Bargaining goes on for
      fifteen minutes. If no settlement is reached, players re-
      turn to strategy session.
   One student should be assigned to keep a record of the
time passing in terms of number of days of the strike.
   To enrich this debate, students should be encouraged to
write a scenario of the company, the union, and the city in
which they are located. Public opinion may be represented as
favoring one or the other party in the conflict depending on the
nature of the city or town. (This is easily done if a public service such as bus transportation is involved.) At the end of each
class period, two students might be asked to play reporters
who try to get information on the progress of negotiations.

Players have no obligation to give out information or to tell the truth.

Scoring. Winner of the game is the team that has come closest to its stated objectives. Labor subtracts from the annual salary of $20 per day times the number of days of the strike. If an additional week's vacation is obtained, the team adds $100. For example, if labor secures $5460 plus one extra week's vacation after three days of the strike, total for the team is $5560 − $60 = $5500. In this situation, management pays $5460 plus $100 = $5560. Since the strike only lasted three days, and management can hold out without loss for five days, $5560 is the total for that team.

Game Adaptability

It is easier to complicate matters than to simplify them, and for that reason teachers of older students have greater flexibility in adapting games originally designed for younger students. Inevitably a game designer discovers that his first version of a game needs to be simplified.

Changing the Level of Difficulty — an Example

Three versions of the game of Neighborhood have been designed. The intention was to provide a simple game for elementary school students who could play intermediate and complex versions of it later in the school year as their course work enabled them to handle more difficult problems. A description of the three versions illustrates the possibilities for adding variables to make a game suitable for older students.

The game is designed to simulate the development of an urban area, based on the settlement and growth of Boston's North End. It is played by four teams of one to three players each. The game is played on a grid board. Each team, represented by different colored chips, place a number of chips on the board each cycle. These represent housing units for a population that increases geometrically each cycle. For every specific number of population pieces, the team must also provide a factory, a store, and a cultural center. As the board becomes more crowded, students may wish to pay for clearing marshland or forest.

The intermediate version is complicated by identifying each population piece by social class. Thus each team has poor, middle-class, and rich pieces. There still remains the basic objective of keeping a team's population together, but in this case new constraints are introduced. If rich players are housed close to a factory, the team loses points. If poor players are housed far from the factory, which is assumed to be their place of work, the team loses points. No one team has complete control over the location of industrial and commercial centers, and one team may move a factory into a rich neighborhood previously set up by another team. In this version, students learn how social classes tend to segregate near the specific items they find desirable.

The advanced version of the game is probably sufficiently complex to be used with college students in city-planning courses. Here, transportation systems and zoning regulations must be legislated for the urban area. Building upwards to house a large population and buying and selling land are permitted. While these actions are permissible in the simpler versions of the game, they are most likely to be employed in the advanced version. The game does not have to stop here. It is possible to specify the commodities produced by the factories and develop an operating economic system in context of the game. Tensions between ethnic groups can be specified, and political figures with different ethnic constituencies can be introduced. Crises, such as the threat of an airport in the center of the area or financial difficulties that require a new tax structure, can be added to the game. Within the basic rule structure, more complications can be added. It is suggested that the most valuable way to complicate the game is to play the basic game with students and solicit their ideas. They can then develop the necessary rules and materials, testing the feasibility of their ideas by actually playing their own, new version of the game.

Custom-tailoring Games

The teacher may wish to adapt games for purposes other than difficulty level. For example, an appropriate game for a particular unit might not be available. Very often an existing game can be changed to give it a different slant. Suppose the class is studying urban transportation. A game such as Section (in which regions of a state compete for funds for projects) could easily be adaped for use with the unit. Instead of vying for the projects specified in the game (hospitals, retraining programs, for example), the sections could ask for highways, rapid transit systems, and other transportation improvements. The game's focus would thus shift to the development of transportation with the state.

As the teacher explores the game technique, he will find that the materials are rewardingly flexible. He will soon discover his own methods of tailoring games to his specifications — just as he already adapts text materials to the specific needs, interests, and abilities of his classes.

CHAPTER 6

THE PROBLEM OF EVALUATION

6

Some Recent Research

Suggestions for Further Research

Practical Considerations for the Teacher

The advocate of educational games urges their use with descriptions of their obvious success. He has seen classrooms of busy, articulate, motivated students. He has listened with delight as students explained complex processes with ease and obvious understanding. Very likely, he has marveled at the sudden participation of the "slow" student. He is firmly convinced that he detects among bright students a deep involvement in games, quite unlike a seemingly superficial, mechanical behavior observed under other conditions. And persuasion to this point of view is nearly irresistible once the skeptic has himself observed several games being played.

But the staunchest advocate of educational games falters when asked to support his enthusiasm with hard proof that games are effective. If asked to demonstrate that games not only are effective but are better than conventional media, the enthusiast pales. Intuitive judgment would be inadequate as the sole basis for embracing a new technique, yet the value of intuition should not be discounted. Game designers are the first to admit that little precise research has yet been done; they are using hunches, intuition, and subjective observations as hints toward developing a research tool for evaluating the effectiveness of games.

As Boocock and Schild noted,[1] the game designers are in the peculiar position of having a technology, or applied science, before the theoretical science has been developed. While most observers would agree that games do teach, what they teach and why are yet to be precisely measured. Educators are in the ironic situation of having found an answer without knowing the question.

Several factors help explain the lack of sound evaluation for educational games. First is the relative newness of the technique, with a consequent lack of time for collecting data and developing systematic evaluation procedures. More serious is the inherent problem of evaluating any technique in education. It is extremely difficult to establish experimental controls — for the variations in the student test populations and particularly for the variations in teachers' personalities, methods, and rapport with students. Even more serious is the fact

[1] Sarane S. Boocock and E. O. Schild, Editors, *Simulation Games in Learning,* *Beverly Hills, Calif.: Sage Publications, 1968.*

that a measuring instrument does not exist. The work done so far has made one point obvious: Standard types of tests are grossly inadequate for measuring whatever it is that games do teach. On the whole, research to date is probably more significant for identifying the difficulites of evaluating games than for precise findings.

Some recent attempts at evaluation are presented here, for they are instructive despite their inadequacy. Suggestions for further research are included, and the practical classroom problem of evaluating student performance is discussed. But the question still looms: "Are games as effective as other teaching tools, or more so?" The answer, at present, must be "We simply do not know."

Some Recent Research

Project SIMILE

In 1965–66, the Western Behavioral Sciences Institute explored the use of simulations with selected social studies classes in junior and senior high schools. Forty simulation trials involving 2500 students were made in seventeen schools. Napoli, Plans, and the Inter-Nation Simulation (all described in Chapter 3) were used with both junior and senior high students; BMG, a business management game, was used with senior high students only.

The objectives of the WBSI study were limited. The researchers wished to determine, broadly, whether or not simulations were feasible within the constraints of the ordinary classroom, and to develop hypotheses about the educational value of simulations.

The study was conducted with an atypical population. The participating teachers were nominated by their principals to attend a workshop that preceded the project and they were paid for doing so. This method of selection led researchers at WBSI to believe that the teacher group was an exceptional one. Similarly, most of the students in the simulations were considered above-average, although this judgment was based mainly on teachers' reports.[2]

To begin the study, WBSI staff members played the games with the teachers who were going to use them. Once the teachers were acquainted with the operation of the simulations, the WBSI staff let teachers run the games on their

---

[2] Hall T. Sprague and R. Garry Shirts, *Exploring Classroom Uses of Simulations,* Project SIMILE, Western Behavioral Sciences Institute, October 1966.

own; however, staff members were available to aid teachers or students if questions arose.

Evaluation of the study depended on information obtained from observations by the WBSI staff, a student questionnaire, and interviews with teachers. Some of the results obtained from the student questionnaires follow.

1. Junior high students rated simulations, as an educational experience, more favorably than senior high students.

2. Junior high and senior high students preferred different simulations. Previous experience with other simulations, the order in which the simulations were used, and other factors might account for the difference; or different age groups might, in fact, respond differently to various types of simulations.

3. Students' own judgments about what they had learned were varied, but tended to fall into one broad category. Statements tended to be generalizations, usually about attitudes toward or opinions about the process being simulated, or about procedural skills of the process being simulated (such as negotiating). Few responses were overall summaries of the basic simulated process. In some cases this result surprised the researchers (who emphasize the necessity for discussing what students think they have learned, since that may prove very different from what the designer or the teacher expects).

The staff of Project SIMILE had the collective hunch that games convey a kind of gutsy learning. When asked, "What did you learn from the simulation?" students rarely responded with factual data, or with essay-test explanations of what caused an event or how a process works. Yet the responses suggest that participants may intuit a process and, without describing it, make judgments that indicate they understood it.

In terms of their own modest goals, the researchers concluded that the use of games is feasible within the existing constraints of the school system. Furthermore, they noted that games are motivating to students and that they lead to further inquiry into the real-world operation of the simulated process.

Critique. The researchers of Project SIMILE themselves admitted various problems in their evaluation procedure. First, their test group was atypical. Second, by their direct participation in the simulations, they probably conveyed their own enthusiasm to teachers and students alike. Third, the training of teachers in advance of play, and the availability of help from the researchers during play, would probably remove any serious element of threat, which a new medium often carries for teachers.

In addition, the nature of the simulations used would be likely to predetermine the kind of student responses about learning. Since the simulations were about encompassing and broad processes—for example, international relations, the legislative process, the U.S. economy—students could be expected to make very general comments about some aspect of the simulation. Unless a postgame discussion preceded the questionnaire, which does not seem to have been the case, no student could be expected to grasp the entire process. Further, since the questionnaire stated "List two or more things you learned from the simulation," students would be likely to mention only general items and unlikely to analyze or describe a process.

The researchers' feeling that learning from games is gutsy is commonly confirmed by observers. Yet this really should be no surprise. Lectures and textbooks rarely convey information about a process in distinct pieces occurring all at the same time. If a process such as legislation is described, it is generally outlined step by step. Games, on the other hand, generally leave the task of synthesizing the various steps in a process to the players themselves. Further, textbooks and lectures, even where they describe incidents or anecdotes about human participants in a process, rarely convey a generalized understanding of the subtle pressures that operate. These pressures and other intangible aspects of human interaction are reproduced in a game, and students tend to develop opinions and judgments of the type they usually make about their own experiences in the real world.

The Project SIMILE study was useful in confirming on a large scale earlier hunches about games as motivating and process-oriented teaching tools. It also helped to confirm that games tend to teach something different from what lectures and textbooks convey. This fact remains the most serious obstacle to any rigorous evaluation of games. Standard tests and research designs are suitable for conventional learning, and a new type of procedure is necessary to determine what games teach and how. An examination of a few other attempts at evaluation will further demonstrate this problem.

Section: A Test Play

The evaluation of the game of Section, developed by Abt Associates Inc. for the High School Geography Project, was even more limited in purpose and procedure than the study carried out by Project SIMILE. The game (described in Chapter 3) was designed to fit into a unit on political geography and this, in turn, was one unit in a year's curriculum in geography. Briefly, the game focused on a hypothetical state whose geographical sections compete and cooperate to obtain a portion of the state budget for public projects that would benefit them.

About 450 students, mostly at the high school level, participated in the game. Since the game was optional in the unit,
teachers who decided to use it constituted, by self-selection,
an atypical group. According to the results available to the
designer, student ability levels varied, although precise data
about these variations was not included. Questionnaires were
distributed to students and teachers, but a fair length of time
elapsed between game play and receipt of the questionnaire.
This time lapse, strictly unintentional, presented some problems
for several teachers, and students commented that they would
have been able to answer more fully if they had received the
questionnaire immediately after play.

The major purpose of this evaluation was to find out if the
game worked. Since the game was designed to last for five or
six class periods and was to be played by thirty students, testing
the game was difficult to arrange outside a regular classroom
situation. The study of Section was primarily an operational
test, rather than an evaluative one, and was intended to point
up procedural bugs in the game.

Some questions of feasibility and ease of administration were
included, however. Teachers were asked whether the scoring
procedures were clear, whether the rules contained enough
information to enable them to run the game "cold," and what
preparation time was required and how this compared with
their ordinary schedule. Teachers were also asked to indicate
any additional substantive information they thought was necessary or desirable for the players to have, and to describe any
difficulties that arose during the game.

Two other types of questions were included for the teacher:
(1) questions about student performance, student response to
losing, and student involvement; (2) questions about how
familiar students were with the concepts treated by the game
prior to play, and estimates of what was learned from the game.
The question about learning from the game was also included
in the student questionnaire.

The results of the evaluation were used in revising the game.
For example, it was discovered that the game was unintention-
ally weighted in favor of the team playing the residents of the
capital city. Because that team had only two projects to request, they usually received money for both. Since the scoring
mechanism provided extra rewards for obtaining more than
one project, or all desired projects, the capital-city team won
too often. In the revised version, the team had more projects
to request and the total state budget was reduced to provide
an additional squeeze on the legislature, which faced more
requests than it could possibly satisfy.

But most important to the designers were the responses students and teachers made to the question of what was learned from the game. In general, the teacher and the student responses emphasized bargaining, negotiation, and compromise as necessary elements in political decision making. Most students also indicated the difficulty of satisfying everyone. Few remarks described reasons for differences between groups. Perhaps this was accepted without question as the structure of the game itself; or students may have already learned, from other parts of the unit, the relation between political processes on the one hand, and economic resources and interests on the other.

Critique. Making an evaluation was a secondary objective in the attempt to remedy any technical problems in the game. The evaluation was only a rudimentary attempt to obtain information from a fairly large test population so that rough comparative judgments could be made about student and teacher perceptions of what was learned; the users' assessments could then be compared with the actual teaching objectives of the game.

Variation in teacher and student perceptions were expected to be minimal, since the questionnaire was distributed after the game was discussed in class. In fact, most teachers indicated that their discovery of what students learned came from postgame discussions. Any major differences in student and teacher responses, then, might be attributed to the greater sophistication of the teachers. Also, the element of retention was not accounted for, since no questionnaire was distributed immediately after play. Student responses about what they had learned might have used vocabulary more closely resembling the teacher's if less time had elapsed between game play and the questionnaire. Even with the time lapse, responses did not differ significantly for the two groups.

If circumstances had allowed, the evaluation of Section might have been used to compare the learning of those students who used the game as part of the geography unit with those who did not. Unfortunately, a thorough procedure was not possible at the time.

Interesting results might have been yielded if another facet had been thoroughly explored. This was an attempt to discover how students related the game to the rest of the unit. The question "What did you learn from the game?" would indicate to students that they confine their answers strictly to the game. Whether they could actually isolate game learning from what they learned elsewhere in the unit is not precisely known from the questionnaires. Half the teachers who used the game were asked whether students were already familiar with the concepts and processes presented. Two-thirds of the group said no; but no full-scale attempt was made to clarify the basis of the teachers' remarks; for example, teachers were not asked specifically if students knew the definition of the concepts in the rest of the unit. Therefore, no significant conclusions could be drawn regarding the aspect questioned.

The nature of the question "What did you learn from the game?" betrays the designers' expectation that what is learned is different from what is learned from textbooks and lectures. It would be interesting to phrase this kind of question in terms similar to those of ordinary tests. Teachers never ask students "What did you learn from Chapter 22 or Lecture 7?" If they did, the responses might be as vague as those elicited by the game questionnaire. On the other hand, if students who played a game were asked to describe a step-by-step process, a better indication of differences between game and nongame learning might be obtained. For example, students who study the legislative process with the traditional "how a bill becomes a law" chart and students who participate in a game simulating the legislative process might profitably be given the same test. It would be reasonable to expect significant differences in responses because the two media tend to emphasize different aspects of and approaches to the topic, but such a test might make it easier to isolate and identify the differences.

Nova Academic Games Project

One of the most promising of recent experiments is the Nova Academic Games Project directed by Professor James Coleman at Johns Hopkins University. The Nova Project is a long-term effort whose goals include the integration of academic games into the curriculum; the evaluation of games in terms of student comprehension, recall, analysis, and synthesis of subject matter; the dissemination of the games, including a teacher-training program that employs videotape. A central part of the program is the use of games as competitive exercises between class teams and school teams. Nova has even conducted Academic Games Olympics, in which teams from several states have participated. The desire to adapt athletic modes to academic endeavors is part of a deliberate attempt to change attitudes toward learning.

The Nova Academic Games Project has described some very impressive evaluation statistics. In an early study conducted in Burbank, California, in 1964, forty-three junior and senior high school students participated in the game of Wff'n Proof,[TM] designed to teach logic. The Nova Project reports that after three weeks of intensive exposure to the game, these students achieved an average increase of 20.9 points in nonverbal IQ. This figure was considered significantly greater than the 6.6 point increase by the control group.

During the same four-month period, eighty-four students in the ninth grade used the game of Equations, designed to teach basic mathematics. These students showed an average increase of 1.3 years in arithmetic reasoning, and this figure was considered significantly greater than the .6 year increase of the control group.

Another study was conducted at Bethel Park Elementary School in Allegheny County, Pennsylvania. During a nine-week period in 1966, a group of 102 fourth-, fifth-, and sixth-grade students participated in playing the game of Equations. During the test period the game was used once a week, for fifty minutes each time; regular text work was used the other four days. Before the study began, students were given the Iowa Test of Basic Skills, Form 1. At the end of the nine weeks, students were given Form 2 of the Iowa Test.

The group as a whole averaged a 5.5-month increase in Arithmetic Concepts Understanding and a 5.9-month increase in Arithmetic Problem Solving Skills — approximately double their usual average increase during a nine-week period.

As indicated by the pretest, the test population had a higher rate of learning of mathematics than normal even before playing the games. But the increase was nevertheless much higher than would have been expected without use of the games. The Nova staff felt that further use of the games would have produced even more significant results.

Critique. These statistical results are extraordinary and encouraging. While a control group is mentioned in the first study, the nature of that group and the experimental procedure is not described. In the second study, no control group is indicated, but student scores are compared with expected scores based on the rate of learning derived from pretest data. Further information about the basis of predicted scores would be desirable.

The apparent precision of these tests can be partly attributed to the precise subject matter of the games and to the existence of ready-made tests to measure mathematical and logical skills. Whether any other kind of intensive drill would have produced the same test results remains in question. If the games still produced higher test scores than a novel technique used with a control group, the question would still be open whether the games were better teaching tools or whether they provided better motivation to learn. The latter result would still stand as impressive testimony to the effectiveness of games, but the reason for their success could be more precisely identified.

It may be in the area of mathematics that precise evaluation of games will be accomplished. The skills to be taught are easier to define, and certainly easier to measure, than the concepts and processes of the social sciences. Because of the differences between the two subject areas, however, evaluation in the mathematics field may be of only marginal value to the social science area.

One point becomes obvious. Suppose the Nova researchers had asked "What did you learn from the game?" after students had played one. Might they have not received the inconclusive, rather useless reply, "I learned how to make equations"? Instead, students in the Nova tests were asked to apply skills learned from the game to new problems. The approach of the Nova Project, partly determined by the subject matter of the games used, offers instructive clues for game evaluation in other areas, particularly the social sciences.

The Johns Hopkins Study

Dr. James Coleman and Dr. Sarane Boocock, of the Department of Social Relations at Johns Hopkins University, have come up with some intriguing, if inconclusive, findings in evaluating the effects of several games they had designed (described in Chapter 3).

One large-scale test was conducted in 1964 at a conference of California 4-H Club members in Berkeley, California. Twelve hundred youngsters, ranging in age from thirteen to twenty-one, participated in one of two games. Career and Legislation were the games used. All the participants were asked to fill out questionnaires both before and after playing a game. The researchers intended each group to act as a control for the other; since each would participate in a game activity, differences in response would not be attributable to the game's novelty for one group. The study made no attempt to compare games with other teaching methods or to control for different types of students, since the overwhelming majority of players claimed to be in the top half of their classes. Several months later, a follow-up test play was run at a 4-H conference in Washington, D.C. A group of 256 youngsters participated in the game of Disaster; no control group was used.

A notable aspect of these studies was the use of structured questions, instead of the open-ended "What did you learn?" employed in other evaluations. Participants in the Career game were asked, for example, to list occupations open to persons of different educational backgrounds, or to itemize the elements contributing to success in marriage. Participants in the legislative game were also asked specific questions; for example, whether pressure groups are useful in representative government.

The researchers noted that all participants in a game tend to acquire a feeling for the process simulated and an appreciation of its complexity. Players also tend to gain confidence that they can do something to control their own lives. For example, the group that played Legislation was more likely than the control group to disagree with the statement that people have no say in government. Further, students seemed to acquire a broader view of the simulated process. The data supporting this contention is admittedly impressionistic, but the Career game participants, for example, tended to mention more items than the control group when asked to describe what position they would like to be in fifteen years in the future.

Critique. The results of the Johns Hopkins study are encouraging though of limited use. That students learn something from games seems clear. However, had each group been given a case study or other printed material, or a lecture on the subjects of careers and legislation—within the same experimental framework—the results might not have been significantly different.

The area of most fruitful research seems to be that for which only impressionistic data is available. Control over the environment, opinions and feelings about the simulated process, and appreciation of complexity might well prove to be unique products of game learning. The significance of these elements needs to be explored, particularly the attitudinal aspect of creating a feeling of control over one's environment and what that might mean for the success of the individual in the real world.

Suggestions for Further Research

Previous research has demonstrated some of the problems impeding the development of a sound evaluation procedure for games. First, the game approach is by nature open-ended. Any rigid list of what students should learn is incompatible with both the purpose and the operation of the game.

Second, processes simulated by games are dynamic, with many variables operating at one and the same time. It is unrealistic to try to determine whether or not students understand the entire process prior to a discussion that permits synthesis of the various players' perceptions. But once such a discussion is conducted, test conditions are tainted and it becomes more difficult to isolate what students have learned from the game as distinct from what they have learned from the teacher. This particular problem need not be insurmountable, for the game and discussion ought to be considered a total experience. However, teacher behavior then becomes critical, and this is enormously difficult to establish controls for.

Third, and most important, is the fact that games are usually designed to teach processes that are inadequately treated in text form or are not treated at all. A game on legislation probably would not be created simply to animate the "how a bill becomes a law" chart, but rather to emphasize aspects of legislation that textbooks cannot convey well. The understanding that games teach different things from lectures and texts has occasionally distorted the evaluation procedure. Often, the researcher faces the dilemma of sensing a difference, but not knowing exactly what the difference is. He tends to ask "What did you learn?" in the hope that the precise differences between games and other media will be revealed. This question can be useful as a preliminary technique, but it has obvious limitations.

For a more realistic assessment of what students learn from games, a comparative study might be worth attempting. An example is a study, conducted among college students, in which one group played the Inter-Nation Simulation while another group studied the same material through case studies. The results of that study indicated few significant differences in interest and achievement; the differences that did exist were not always favorable to the game.

The study made no attempt to identify what distinguished the game from other methods used. But this line of inquiry might well be pursued. In an experimental setup, one group of students could use a series of case studies to explore elements of legislation usually ignored in texts; at the same time a game could serve to teach roughly the same thing to another group. One or more control groups would be necessary. To account for the novelty of playing a game, which would possibly be only a temporary motivation, a third group of students would have to be taught the process of legislation through an equally novel technique with no case study or game enrichment. All the groups would have the same objective — to define the process of legislation in terms the researchers identified — and a test would have to be devised to elicit responses on the subject from participants. If significant differences occurred often enough in testing, the source of the differences between methods might be isolated. A longitudinal study would also be important in an experiment of this kind. Retention of what is learned from games may differ significantly from other media, a facet that has not yet been thoroughly tested.

Probably the best kind of test to administer to groups using different methods would be one that tested transfer. This would consist of a problem-solving exercise, different in content from the game or case studies, but requiring the application of the same skills and process-oriented knowledge that students were supposed to learn from each. One of the key values of games seems to be that they develop problem-solving abilities more effectively than other media, and a study directed at testing this hypothesis would be worthwhile. A fact-oriented test, on the other hand, would measure the basic minimum learned by all groups, without exploring the upper limits of what was learned. Such a test might be useful, however, to determine whether students who used process-oriented case studies fared significantly better than game participants; these two groups could also be compared with a third control group. Tests of transfer should be used at various points in such an experiment, immediately before the study of a process began, immediately after, and at several subsequent intervals.

An evaluation like the one described would be enormously difficult to set up because of the inherent difficulties of matching students and teachers, and because of the expense and difficulty of constructing specially matched materials in a variety of media. The experiment would, however, serve to identify any real differences in the kind of learning that games produce. If no significant differences were produced in a sound procedure, the hunch that games are important for *how* rather than *what* they teach might prove to be the key distinction between games and other media.

Practical Considerations for the Teacher

The inadequacy of evaluation research to date should not hinder teachers from using educational games. We may not know whether games are actually more effective than other media. But we do know that games are usually designed to teach processes that other media may not attempt to teach. The first question the teacher faces is whether or not any other media exists to teach the stated objectives of the game, rather than which will teach it better. Often, games have a monopoly on teaching a particular process.

The novelty and the motivational aspects of games, which concern researchers who wish to develop a purely comparative evaluation procedure, certainly do not worry the teacher. If games motivate, or even if games motivate only when they are new to the class, then make the most of it.

Long-term research might prove that the value of games lies more in their capacity to influence attitudes than in their ability to convey substantive information. In this event, the medium will prove to be even more worthwhile than if its function were restricted to teaching facts. Nobody suggests that games should be used all the time to teach all things. But if they are as effective in altering attitudes as intuition suggests, all other media can be utilized more effectively. One of the most promising leads in past research is that games give students a feeling that control over their environment is possible. Results of investigation into this aspect of games is eagerly awaited.

In-class Evaluation

If the teacher decides to use games despite the limited scientific knowledge about them, he then faces the question of how to evaluate student performance in the activity. First, no evaluation is worth doing prior to the postgame discussion in which students and teacher participate. Evaluating what students have learned from the game itself might consist of an essay describing the total process, whether that is legislation, trade under a mercantilist system, the principle of supply and demand, or the polarization of loyalties on a political issue.

Probably more useful than a description would be a problem that required students to apply what they learned in the game. For example, a number of real or hypothetical people might be described and students asked to predict which side in a controversy each would have chosen and why. Or, students might be asked to extrapolate price fluctuations in a market situation, given such data as number of buyers, recent prices, utility of the commodity. Presented with a situation of persistent violation of trade rules on the part of colonists, students might be asked to plan strategies for the mother country. In another case, students might be asked to explain how they themselves would go about passing legislation they desired, given a brief sketch of the characteristics and sentiments of the rest of the legislature. Or they might be given a legislative procedure that differed from the game's, with the task of developing a fitting strategy for passing legislation. This alternative would give students an opportunity to apply such basic functions as negotiation and bargaining, which exist apart from procedural variations.

It is hoped that postgame tests would be used for diagnostic purposes — to discover what students have learned and where they are weak — and not for grades. With the suggested evaluations, no single response is necessarily the only or the best one, and students' strategies could be discussed and judged by their peers. Such tests will not yield precise grades; but conventional media offer enough opportunity for grading students in the usual fashion. Games are best used in the context of an entire curriculum, for what has been learned from games will contribute to and be reinforced in other media. Direct testing for games is thus unnecessary for grading purposes.

Indirect benefits of games may appear in other tests, through increased understanding of a subject as well as increased motivation to study it. This effect should apply to standardized tests, too, and any concern that students who use games will not fare as well on such tests would seem to be unfounded.

The only valid basis for concern is merely the matter of allocating classroom time. If students spend time playing games in class, teachers may feel concern that the standard course of study will not be covered. However, observers have noted frequent instances of students actually volunteering to do more homework so they could use games in class. In this event, the teacher can reinforce and ensure the learning of regular course material by introducing it into discussions about the game. Currently, many games are being developed explicitly for integration into a total curriculum—making it easy for the teacher to relate game and text learning, since the two are designed for concurrent use. Often, exercises requiring application of learning from different media are included in the curriculum itself.

In short, no major problem of evaluation confronts the classroom teacher. When tests of learning transfer are designed for research evaluation purposes, the teacher's task of constructing such instruments will be diminished. For the time being, it would seem a worthwhile effort for the teacher to develop them for his own class. Perhaps it would be even better to have the class develop its own postgame exercises. To construct hypothetical situations using the principles of the game would be an educational experience in itself, one impossible without real learning. Peer evaluation of both the problems presented and solutions developed would undoubtedly be the best method of evaluation.

CHAPTER 7

GAMES AND ATTITUDES

7

Games for Exploring Attitudes

Classroom Applications

Heroes and Scholars

One of the most promising hunches about educational games is that they can influence and alter the attitudes of participants. Specifically, this hunch applies to three areas. First, games can evidently be used to change attitudes about the particular issue a game treats. Second, and even more encouraging, experience with educational games can apparently improve participants' attitudes toward learning and the school system in general. Third, games appear to influence the student's attitude about his own effectiveness in his environment.

Of all the aspects of educational games, the effect on attitudes is the most elusive. Measuring changes in any attitude is difficult. It is not surprising that the little research that has been done about games and attitudes has yielded results that are inconclusive at best. Yet many researchers are convinced that the primary value of games lies in their ability to improve attitudes. They have personally witnessed the flourishing of the withdrawn student, the socialization of the aggressive student, the cooperativeness of the disruptive student. Many people in the field find that observations of these phenomena are often more convincing than test results, which may fail to record such changes.

For the teacher, researchers' hypotheses about games and attitudes suggest some practical classroom applications. Attitudes are among the most difficult things to explore and teach—whether these are the attitudes prevalent in another culture or historical period under study, or the students' own attitudes concerning such matters as cultural differences, the value of education, or their acceptance by peers. Games can well be used for the task, to aid in socializing students or as a tool for exploring substantive, if intangible, concepts.

Included in this chapter are suggestions for the use of games to teach attitudes, to elevate the value of scholastic achievement, and to increase the student's feeling of effectiveness in his environment. The simple games and exercises dealing with the students' attitudes are in no way intended to be psychological research or therapy. They are samples of effective formats for discussing attitudes that influence behavior; they demonstrate an approach that permits the students to make their own judgments, while enabling the teacher to avoid preaching and moralizing.

Games for Exploring Attitudes

Changing an individual's attitude toward anything is enormously difficult. Even teaching about the attitudes of other cultures is a challenging task. While students may repeat appropriate responses on tests, intellectual acceptance or understanding of an attitude may have no influence at all on the individual's behavior. A student may learn thoroughly the sources and characteristics of prejudice; yet that student's behavior may exhibit all the signs of prejudice, with no promise of change. Attitudes are not formed or expressed in intellectual terms; essentially they are aspects and qualities of emotional life.

Altering an attitude requires that the individual first comprehend it fully on its emotional as well as on its intellectual levels. Attitudes are not remade or cultivated in one grandiose stroke, of course. But a teacher can help students examine personal views by providing classroom situations in which the implications and effects of particular attitudes can be played out.

Teaching attitudes through the use of games resembles the classic use of role playing as an opportunity to try out behavior—a technique widely used for training, education, and psychotherapy. The behavior may be the individual's own response in a defined situation or a behavior assigned to him. In psychotherapy, an individual is sometimes asked to act out, with the therapist, a problem that is disturbing him; afterwards, he attempts to analyze the responses he made in the role-playing situation. In group therapy or study sessions a situation may be defined by the group leader, acted out by a few participants, and discussed by the actors and observers alike.

For education or training, role playing is used almost invariably to convey intangible elements of a process or skill. Basically, the role-play technique permits practice in interpersonal skills, which conventional media can only describe with limited effect. Sales training provides a typical example: Trainees try to sell to their colleagues and the players mutually evaluate their interaction with the aim of improving performance.

The use of simulations and games to teach or alter attitudes has been receiving increasing attention in the selection and training of personnel. Some recent applications in education, nursing, government, and industry illustrate this trend.

Teacher Training

Attitudes of education students were the target of an experiment at Oregon College of Education. The researchers hoped to determine whether the use of teaching simulations would help improve students' attitudes toward the content of education courses. For purposes of the study, the researchers assumed that the students' slightly negative attitude derived from the failure to perceive the relevance of course content to actual teaching practices. Since any attempt to provide real classroom experience seemed to be both impractical and potentially traumatic in the early stages of training, twenty students were confronted with typical problems of a hypothetical sixth grade, presented in audiovisual form. Each education student was asked to observe the problem and respond to it; he then received feedback describing the most likely consequence of the behavior he exhibited toward a student or the class.

The researchers attempted to measure differences in attitude between the experimental group that used the simulation, and the control group that did not. However, pregame and postgame tests revealed little significant difference, at least statistically. The researchers attributed the uniformity of results to two factors: the inadequacy of the attitude-measurement test, and the fact that the students' initial attitudes were more positive than anticipated. Nevertheless, the experimental group did show an improvement in attitude after using the simulation. Despite the relative insensitivity of the attitude tests, the researchers felt that the simulation was a valuable means of enhancing attitudes toward education courses by making the content more relevant to future teachers.

Nursing

Nursing is another area where there is a great need for training in interpersonal skills and attitudes. Some schools of nursing have considered the use of simulations and games to provide student nurses with practice in the nontechnical, nonmedical aspects of patient care.

One basic simulation, under development, is designed to increase the sensitivity of student nurses to the social and psychological needs of patients. Student nurses play the roles of nurses, head nurses, administrators, and patients. In the course of a simulated 24-hour day, players are asked to tend to the needs of patients with different medical conditions, as well as different socioeconomic and ethnic backgrounds. Patient profiles include such information as family problems and personal disappointments ("Unless you are released from the hospital within two days, you will miss your son's college graduation. You worked as a waitress for four years to put him through—it's your day as much as his and you are determined to see it"). Conflicts among the patients in the ward are built into the simulation. The student nurses playing patients are asked to evaluate the effectiveness of their fellow students (playing hospital personnel) in identifying their problems and dealing with them. The roles are then reversed.

The simulation rests on the fundamental hypotheses that skill with people cannot be learned from books and lectures. While only a few individuals are fortunate enough to have an instinctive understanding and ability (the proverbial bedside manner), role playing can develop such skills; it helps student nurses empathize with the patient by permitting them to play that role as well as to practice their own.

Cross-cultural Training

A similar problem confronts agencies engaged in training civilian personnel for overseas work. Lectures about the characteristics of another culture are insufficient to prepare Americans for living and working with an unfamiliar people. Eating native food, learning to play native games, studying a foreign political structure, and practicing the language are usually inadequate to enable the trainee to operate effectively in a foreign land. Most difficult to convey is an understanding of attitudes that are alien to those of the trainee.

The degree of necessary adaptation can be reduced through simulations and games that provide an opportunity to familiarize individuals with the habits of another culture. Typically, a training group is divided into at least two groups: one representing various native roles, and the other representing the Americans in the roles they will fulfill abroad. In preparing civilian advisers for service in Far Eastern villages, for instance, some trainees are cued to behave as Oriental villagers: sensitive to a particular authority structure, in which the village chief commands respect and loyalty; interested in obtaining food; basically apolitical; suspicious of foreigners. Those trainees who play American advisers and aides often discover that, despite all their reading and homework, their behavior is offensive to the natives. They find that they have less sensitivity to and patience with alien attitudes than they had assumed. This kind of contact with a foreign culture, although artificially structured and induced, increases empathy and usually stimulates a closer scrutiny and analysis of the individual's own behavior and attitudes. The technique is not a substitute for actual contact with the culture, but it does enable the trainee to practice what he probably has accepted intellectually. It thus provides an important means of testing the extent of his training before he begins active duty.

Job Screening

Simulations and games are also effective in the selection of job applicants when attitudes are of critical significance. No matter how impressive an applicant's résumé, references, and interview may be, his performance on the job is still difficult to predict. There is no foolproof method of eliminating this uncertainty, but simulation techniques can be used to reduce it. The applicant's performance in simulated job situations is usually a good indicator of how successful he will be in the actual position. Good performance is a strong support for an outstanding record; poor performance throws serious doubt on an otherwise favorable impression.

In the summer of 1967, a large-scale simulation was held at Abt Associates, Inc. in Cambridge, Massachusetts, for the purpose of evaluating applicants for various positions at a women's Job Corps Center. The activities of a regular 24-hour day were condensed into one and one-half work days. Staff members played the roles of urban and rural Job Corps trainees, interested political officials, male hangers-on, community leaders. Applicants played the positions they were applying for, ranging from Job Corps Director to social studies teachers to guidance counselors. A variety of incidents were crammed into the simulation. A senator visited unexpectedly. A near scandal had reporters snooping. Personal crises and conflicts arose among the women. The assigned troublemakers disrupted activities with great skill. Events programmed by the designers, as well as many that were elicited by profiles but not particularly planned for, occurred with oppressive regularity.

At the end of the simulation, staff participants and staff observers had evaluated all the applicants. In many cases, the applicants role-played themselves out of a job. While the pressure was somewhat exaggerated in intensity, individuals who could not handle the simulated situation were not expected to perform well in the job. The simulation was extremely successful in identifying interpersonal skills and attitudes, and this use of the technique has widespread application in many fields.

A similar though less-structured technique has been used to select applicants for executive positions in business. In the exercise, applicants are presented with a variety of letters, telephone messages, and meeting agenda that an executive might find in his In basket. Within a fixed period, they are to sort out the items competing for their time, and handle them in order of priority. The applicant's success in coping with many business problems, scored according to a predetermined scale of priority, provides a basis for selecting or screening out executives. This exercise, in which players compete with the environment, or a set standard, attempts to identify subtle abilities of judgment and decisiveness.

Classroom Applications

While the exercises described above have been used exclusively with adults, the use of games and simulations has application at the elementary and secondary school level as well. What follows is a set of suggested games for exploring the attitudes of other cultures, and for identifying student attitudes and playing out their implications.

Our Gang: A Game of "Ins" and "Outs"

The peer group is of primary importance to students of secondary-school age, who have great need for acceptance and find rejection by the group extremely painful. The cohesion of the group, which cultivates and reinforces the values of its members, can lead at the same time to severe, irrational actions against outsiders. But the problem of the group is hardly confined to youngsters. Cultural subgroups in our society behave in ways similar to natural friendship cliques. The problem of feeling "in" or "out" or of making others feel "in" or "out" is common to all groups. And the reason for acceptance and rejection in either case is related to a fear of difference and the threat that different values sometimes pose to the existence of a group.

The game Our Gang can be used in a variety of forms to study the nature of a group and the factors that contribute to defining people as "in" or "out."[1] The version that follows treats cultural differences.

Players. Divide the class into two groups of unequal size (approximately two-thirds and one-third of the class). The larger group represents Our Gang and controls jobs, businesses, schools, housing, and other institutions of the community known as Our Place. The smaller group, the Newcomers, represents immigrants to the community. It is a close-knit group with a special language, religion, and social code.

[1]The author wishes to thank Linda Elbow for the design of the game Our Gang.

Assign one or two students to represent the press. To members of Our Gang, assign typical community roles: police chief and two policemen, minister, school principal or teacher or both, mayor and councillors, several storekeepers and businessmen, several workers, and one or two real estate agents. To develop group cohesiveness, encourage students to write a sketch of their own roles, to draw a map of the community, and perhaps to elect their own mayor and town officials. Students should also be encouraged to suggest other roles for the game. As soon as roles have been developed and assigned, convene a town meeting where students elect officials and develop a simple code of rules governing the community. These might include rules about voting requirements, taxes, minimum wage, school attendance. Students should explore the areas for which laws are necessary and decide for themselves how extensive their code should be. At any time during the game, the mayor may reconvene Our Gang and suggest new laws that seem necessary.

Meanwhile, the Newcomers should meet in another part of the room to develop their own code of behavior. A simple speech code (Pig Latin, numbers) can be developed for mandatory use among the members. This group might select a weekday for the observance of their hypothetical religion and agree to adhere to it strictly. (For example, any Newcomer who works on that day will be fined by the group, and will not be spoken to for a simulated day.) Students should be encouraged to make their rules of behavior considerably different from Our Gang's. For this purpose, one Newcomer should be permitted to listen in on the deliberations of Our Gang.

Objectives. The objective of Our Gang is to maintain a well-run community (collect taxes to keep the community in good condition, pay administrative salaries, minimize crime and punish offenders, educate all the children of the community, keep unemployment at zero).

The objective of the Newcomers is to maintain their loyalty to their group (this includes observing their own rules) while functioning in the community—supporting themselves, avoiding trouble with the law.

Action. The action takes place in a series of rounds, or simulated days:

1. The Newcomers should first seek appointments with real estate agents and businessmen in order to find a place to live and work. This should be done in pairs so that Newcomers have an opportunity to converse with each other in their secret code, although they use English with members of Our Gang.

Newcomers should be reminded that they cannot work on one weekday, for religious observance, and this should be told to potential employers. Wages should be negotiated. Employers have the option of conversing to fix wage levels. They may try to persuade Newcomers to work on their terms, for example, to work on all weekdays, despite religious beliefs.

While some Newcomers are seeking employment, the rest are looking for housing. Agents may insist that no housing be rented to Newcomers unless they can prove they have a job, and therefore a means to pay the rent. Once a Newcomer obtains a job, however, the rest of the group may live with him until they too find jobs and can rent their own dwellings.

Allow fifteen to thirty minutes to represent one day. At the end of that time, any Newcomers in Our Gang's part of the room return to their own section.

2. At this stage, points are tallied: *Our Gang:* One negative point for each unemployed resident of Our Place. Five positive points for no crises, or a resolved crisis. *Newcomers:* One negative point for each member who has violated the rules of the group or left it. Two positive points for each member who has obtained employment without compromising the group's code.

3. Meanwhile, the one or two students who represent the press should write news bulletins. These should be announced to all at the end of the simulated day. One might be a brief description of a theft (police and town officials may be notified prior to public announcement). As the next day begins and the Newcomers again set out to find employment and housing, the police may interview anybody at any time to try to discover who committed the crime.

The press should determine in advance that it was either committed by an individual not represented in the game, or secretly negotiate with a member either of Our Gang or the Newcomers to agree to be the offender.

Police should be asked to record their suspicions. At the end of the day, they must announce who they believe committed the theft. If correct, Our Gang scores one point; if not, no score is added.

Another example of a crisis in the community might be a natural disaster such as a flood. The press might state that the entire community is required to work together to repair damage, aid the injured, and otherwise deal with the problem. (Groups of six students, two Newcomers and four Our Gang members, have to work together for a simulated day.) A proportion of the houses may be announced as destroyed; owners of those remaining might be asked to take in flood victims for a simulated day or two.

Winners. Our Gang will win if it has been able to reduce the Newcomers to one-third their original number. (This includes employment on Our Gang's terms.)

The Newcomers will win if they have maintained their group at two-thirds its original size and managed to obtain employment on their terms.

Resources. To tighten the structure of the game, a simple monetary system may be built into it. A basic subsistence cost may be assigned to all players. At the end of each simulated day or week, subsistence costs must be paid. For the Newcomers, a few members of the group should be permitted to pay the subsistence of all, if they can afford it. This permits a few to work and helps the rest avoid compromising the group code. If this subsistence is introduced, scoring on the number of unemployed members of the community is unnecessary; negative points may be tallied only for members who cannot pay subsistence.

Discussion. What players did in the game should be discussed after play. Did the Newcomers compromise their code? What pressures did they feel to do so or not to do so? How did they feel toward Our Gang? Were they treated fairly? How did Our Gang feel toward the Newcomers? Were they able to persuade them to ignore their group and follow the rules of the larger community? Did they turn toward them first when a problem arose in Our Place? How did they feel about the Newcomers conversing in their own language? Did the Newcomers feel closer, special, or isolated because of their language?

What makes an individual feel "in" or "out" of a group? What attributes besides language make an individual identify with one group or another? Can an individual maintain loyalty and uphold the values of one group and still work within another larger, different group? What kinds of groups in our society resemble Our Gang and Newcomers? How are school fraternities similar to and different from the two groups in the game? Do competing football teams resemble or differ from the two groups in the game? Do students have any relatives or neighbors who seem to be more like Newcomers than Our Gang? Do parents and children represent two different groups? Students and teachers?

Variations. The basic concept of the game Our Gang may be modified to treat groups that form within a culture, rather than between cultures.

Divide the class into five groups of approximately six players each. Two students should be assigned to play referees.

Have a referee flash a card before the group. Ask each group to secretly discuss what was on the card. Each member of each group should record his response. The group response (majority or compromise) should be submitted to a referee.

The card should then be shown again. All individuals who identified the subject of the card correctly should form a new group. All other players should be reorganized into four groups of about six players each.

For the next two or three cards, the groups may be reconstituted again. At that point, the groups should remain fixed except that individuals may ask the referee for permission to switch to another group. Transfer should be limited to one or two students per round.

Each group should be identified by name, letter, or number and should score a point for each correct response.

At the end of ten rounds of play, tally not only the score but the number of members of each group. Did the group that gave the first few correct responses increase in size? If so, why? Did students find it desirable to join the winning side?

It may be that no group consistently gives the correct responses at first. In that case, determine the answers for three or four cards; then permit students to change groups. Do not reveal the correct answer for the rest of the cards until written responses have been made for all of them. Ask players why they changed groups. Did they expect a particular group, or some members of a group, to have the right answers most often? Or did they join a group because they felt they agreed with that group, right or wrong, more than they did with their own? Or did they remain with an original group? If so, why?

An Interview Game

A game about job interviewing would be extremely useful for high school students interested in permanent or summer employment. Lectures in class on proper dress and grooming never seem to make a real impact. Practice in rather formal conversation, as might take place in an interview, is rarely available to the student in school or anywhere else. And the key elements — the applicant's and the employer's attitudes — are not usually discussed.

A simple game can be set up in which students play applicants and employers. These roles should be delineated in writing so that individuals are not threatened by an evaluation of their own personal behavior. Rather, they experiment with a type of behavior not necessarily their own. Where there is a similarity, the student will make the connections.

Divide the class into three groups of approximately ten players each. Divide each of the three groups in half, one half to play employers, one to play job applicants. Have the three employer teams develop five profiles describing the personalities of five different employers in five different fields. These should include not only the qualifications the employer hopes to find in an applicant, but the personal peculiarities. ("You would not under any circumstances hire anybody who chewed gum" — camp director, business executive.)

Meanwhile, have the three applicant teams develop five profiles describing the personalities of five prospective employees. These need not be specific as to type of job, but should focus on habits of speech, posture, purpose. ("You really don't want a job at all but unless you work this summer you will be unable to continue school next year. That would be even worse because you'd have to work all year. You're looking for the best-paying, easiest job you can find although you are willing to claim you'll work very hard if that will help you land a job." "You cannot sit long in one position and tend to slouch, but you don't think that should be of any concern to an employer as long as you do your job.")

Within each of the three groups, an applicant should meet with an employer for ten to fifteen minutes, then rotate to the next until all applicants have met with all employers. Employers should use an evaluation form that varies with the job. For example, the camp director looking for counselors is interested in athletic and musical skills, fondness for children, leadership qualities, willingness to take responsibility, and good grooming. The garage owner is looking for mechanical skills, arithmetic skills, and amiability, but is not particularly concerned with leadership, gum chewing, or posture. Each applicant should be encouraged to portray his role even in interviews for jobs he probably would not seek under actual circumstances. At the end of each interview, employers should rate applicants on a scale, or with a plus, minus, or neutral sign. Applicants might record their estimate of what the employer was looking for, what seemed to be pleasing or offensive to the employer, and how they expected the employer to rate them.

These notes should be compared at the end of the game. Roles should then be reversed, giving employers an opportunity to play applicants. New profiles might be developed for the second round.

At the end of the game, students should discuss what qualities or skills seemed most important for different jobs and how personal idiosyncrasies influenced the success or failure of an interview. In accord with his profile, how did a prospective employer feel toward the applicant who chewed gum? Was the employer's opinion affected by the way an applicant sat? Did the employer feel the applicant really wanted to work? On what basis did he make his judgment?

Aim: A Life-style Game

To demonstrate the fundamental importance of attitudes in shaping life styles (these attitudes, in turn, having been shaped by earlier life styles), a simple board game may be constructed.

Sketch out a grid of ten squares by ten squares The first row of ten squares represents a path toward the aim of earning a living. The other nine parallel rows represent the job market. At any point along the first row of ten squares, players may move horizontally into the job market. Or they may choose to continue to ascend up the scale representing higher levels of education and training. The longer a player remains on this investment, or education, scale, the better the job he will qualify for.

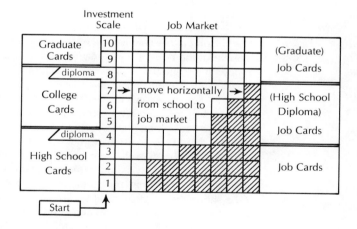

Several sets of cards should be developed. The first applies to the investment scale and should describe a variety of frustrations (and some rewards) related to school (ranging from early high school to graduate training). Players start at square 1 and pick a card. Example: "You think high school is a drag. Some of your friends have already quit and they're making money and have lots of free time. Two of them have already bought the latest model cars. They think you're crazy for staying in school. Will you?" The player may choose to stay at level 1 and wait a turn to pick another card determining the conditions of his moving to level 2. Or the player can move horizontally at level 1 and pick a job card at his next turn. If he chooses the latter, his first level 1 job card may state that "so far, after two interviews, nobody has been willing to hire you. You're flat broke but will keep trying. Or do you want to go back to school?" The player can then wait at job market, at level 1, in the hope that his next card will bring better luck; or he can return to the investment scale, at level 1, and hope for easy advancement in school. If he stays in school instead of going into the job market, or returns to school after a frustrating experience outside, his next card might say "You have flunked algebra, which you need in order to graduate. Will you take it again this summer or give up entirely?"

Six sets of cards are needed:

1. high school cards
2. college cards
3. graduate cards
4. job cards — no high school diploma
5. job cards — high school diploma
6. job cards — college diploma and higher

Some of the college cards may require that students work to pay tuition and thus stay at one level for two or three turns, representing a reduced program. The jobs get progressively better as the player enters the job market at a higher level. Some of the very low level job cards might tempt the player into crime and a jail term (lose two turns). Some advancement upward should be possible through the job market itself. ("You have learned your trade so well you have been promoted. Now you earn as much money as the starting salary of a high school graduate.") On the other hand, the horizontal paths should be blocked off at the lower levels so that maximum advancement is possible across only two or three upper levels. Salaries should increase by a small amount as one moves along a level horizontally, and should increase by a greater amount as one moves up vertically. The big jumps are at the levels of high school diploma and college diploma, which entitle the player to select from a new deck of cards. (The low-level deck should not contain a great many cards.)

The player's own decisions will shape his course in the game. His responses to hard luck, frustration, delay, and other obstacles help determine whether he moves further up the scale or remains in a position that promises relatively little improvement.

The game should be limited to four players, although several games could be used simultaneously by a class. Players should keep a record of their earnings. Each move represents a year and the game continues until the last player has advanced as far as he can. If a player decides to remain at a level, he simply keeps earning, in each subsequent round, the salary shown on the last card he drew out of the deck. The player with the highest total earnings at the end of the game is the winner.

Games for Effective Action

A serious weakness of the school system is the feeling of impotence it induces among students. The system is seen as something that acts on them without being sensitive to their influence in return. The best they can hope to do is respond to the system successfully—but what constitutes success is also imposed by the system itself. The educational game setup is a healthy corrective to this weakness. In playing games, students tend to develop feelings of effectiveness and control because the actions they take in the game produce results. Active participation in decision making increases feelings of influence in an environment.

Besides being dynamic in structure, games treat subjects that are active, real-world processes. As noted in Chapter 6, students who participated in the legislative game tended to disagree more often with the statement that people have no say in government than students who did not play. Participation in a simulated process allows students to explore possible courses of action and discover their effects.

This distinctive advantage of the medium might be nullified unless a deliberate effort is made to relate games to the real world. Games could take on the "some day in the future" tone that colors much course material. To maximize feelings of control over the environment, games should be used, at least occasionally, for developing specific strategies that students can apply to immediate problems. A practical example is the interview game.

Another largely unexplored application of games is in the area of community projects. Elementary school students are usually led to explore their own community. And more and more secondary schools are interested in better community relations, seeking fuller school participation and encouraging the community to use and contribute to the school's resources. Particularly in so-called disadvantaged areas, the need for closer relations between the school and the community is pressing. Failure to reduce the existing isolation of the schools threatens to make the institution anachronistic.

Schools could take the lead in small-scale community improvement. In one community, students voluntarily organized to clean up a deserted lot and turn it into a recreation area. Such a project could usefully be explored in game form first.

In designing the game, property ownership should first be determined. Students and teacher together should then develop a strategy for obtaining permission to use the land for recreation, either from public authorities or a private owner. A variety of community agencies might be enlisted. Local businessmen might be asked to contribute funds or materials for outdoor athletic equipment. Local park authorities might be asked to participate in operating the playground. To develop students' confidence and skill in dealing with adults in the community (some of whom might be expected to be apathetic at best, and perhaps negative), profiles of people in positions of influence should be written. Some students should be asked to play these people while others simply play themselves. An interview session would serve to give students practice in asking the relevant questions, using the arts of persuasion, thinking on their feet, developing alternative suggestions and alternative sources of aid in the event of rejection. Bringing several parents into the game situation would be effective. With luck, one or two influential citizens might be enlisted to aid in developing game strategies, which could be used later in the real situation.

Heroes and Scholars

The heroes of youngsters are rarely scholars. In adolescent society, the athlete is more often respected and rewarded with the approval of his peers. For perhaps a majority of the student populations, the value of school and of academic achievement is imposed and asserted by the school itself, and sometimes by the home. But when the peer group implicitly rejects this value, its impact is seriously reduced, even for the would-be scholar.

The Nova Academic Games Project in Fort Lauderdale, Florida has deliberately attempted to introduce the athletic mode into academic pursuits. The aim is to alter the values and the reward structure in schools so that the academic achiever can receive the same kind of prestige and respect from his peers that the athlete does. In this way, it is hoped that students will be motivated to achieve academic success.

The program is built around a large-scale use of games. Not only are educational games used in the classroom but they provide the focus for competition among classes and even schools. During the summer of 1967, a second Academic

Games Olympics was held at Nova, in which 240 students from eight states participated. The contest received widespread publicity through the local press, radio, and television. Nova looks forward to even greater participation from many schools across the nation. In the future, academic competitions may achieve the proportions and the tenacity of athletic contests as an integral part of the education system.

This effort poses various potential dangers, which the Nova people are aware of themselves. First, the academic competitions must remain broadly based, If they become the area of "eggheads" alone, with the majority of students turned into spectators, the value of such a program could be much diminished. Also, the emphasis on winning in sports is somewhat more acceptable than in academics. The object, after all, is to learn and that goal must not be lost in the motivation to win.

Some important differences exist between educational and athletic games. In educational games, nobody necessarily loses because somebody else wins. Furthermore, the advantage of a finely trained team is not as important in educational games as in athletics. And while winning is the paramount objective of an athletic competition, success in terms of the rules is the emphasis in educational games. Several teams may seek to develop winning strategies in an educational game, but in a sense they are playing mainly against the game and only incidentally against each other.

Educational games also depend less on specialized skill than athletic competitions — with less danger of developing a few stars or heroes. With social science games in particular, competitions might be arranged so that the winning teams within each game are compared with the winning teams in other classes. In that way, even the teams that did not win in an individual classroom would still identify with their class position in, for example, a school-wide contest.

One way of avoiding the dangers of athletic contests while using their advantages is to run contests in game design. The analytic process required in building a game is even more educational than in playing it. As games become more widely used, students should be encouraged to design their own, perhaps for contests at the local, state, or national level. A topic such as "the legislative process" could be selected, and the appropriate grade level could be asked to design a game to simulate it. A project like this provides something for everybody to do — research and analysis, coordination, art work. Each class would test and refine its own game. Each school would run several sessions of testing so that students could play the games that other classes designed. The students themselves would then select the best game to represent their school in the district. Testing many games in one school might prove to be too time consuming; if so, the project could be limited to the design of one game for the entire school, with several classes participating in various aspects of the task. The whole competition would resemble a science fair, with the educational games serving as social science laboratories.

An individual teacher might pursue the idea of competitive game designs by dividing the class into two groups, and having each develop a game about a process under study. A simple example, again, is the legislative process. The topic should first be studied by the whole class; it should be defined clearly so that students have a reasonably sound understanding before proceeding with detailed research. Communication between each group and the teacher should be frequent. Evaluation of each game should be done by the competing team, based on how well the game reflects the legislative process, how seriously any simplifications dis- torted the process, how playable the game is, and whether or not it is fun. This kind of competition would be a very rich learning experience—a great step forward from the spelling bee.

APPENDIXES

GAMES FOR GROWTH

The Game of Fixit

FIXIT (Fostering, or Fighting, Innovations and Experiments in Teaching) is a game for teachers, administrators, and parents.[1] It focuses on the problem of integrating educational innovations, such as games and simulations, into school systems. Such decisions involve numerous tangible and intangible elements that operate in the educational structure and the community. Budgeting of time and money, personalities and personal relations, flexibility of teachers and administrators, educational philosophy, parental concerns, makeup of the school population, and the community's receptivity to change are among the factors that come into play.

The author has designed FIXIT as a means of exploring the nature of the decision-making process. The game also provides players with an opportunity to gauge the sentiments for and against innovation that are likely to emerge in different settings and situations. The game is built around the decision a hypothetical school system must make regarding the introduction of educational games. Several school profiles are included, and players may employ any one of the different descriptions. Players are encouraged to play the game more than once, using a different school profile each time.

The game of FIXIT is set on the eve of a school's budget preparation. One of the items to be discussed is a request for funds to introduce game materials on an experimental basis. The proposal has drawn considerable attention from staff members, since implementing it would probably mean that funds in another area of the budget would have to be cut. While the game does not explore financial pressures in detail, it does give players an opportunity to express their views for and against such a plan. Personal conflicts, personal ambitions, and attitudes toward education are brought into play.

After a negotiating session, during which each player has an opportunity to talk to every other player, a vote is taken for or against the experimental program. Every player wishes to persuade the others to vote with him. Whether or not a school system introduces games into its curriculum depends on the majority vote. (The votes are not equal, however. For example, administrators' votes are heavily weighted.)

The game has no single winner. Winning players are those whose preference is adopted by the school system.

---

[1] The author wishes to thank Barbara Harris for her aid in developing the game of FIXIT.

Game materials include the player profiles and school profiles provided on the following pages. The only other materials required are pencils and paper.

Rules

For the next hour or two, you will play the role of teacher,
school administrator, or parent in a particular school system.
(The school profile should be chosen by the group as a whole.)
The question at issue is whether or not to introduce games into
your schools. You need not consider what kinds of games, or
how many. The only question that must be decided now is
whether or not you will plan to use games in the coming school
year. Since the school budget must be prepared, your decision
must be made now so that money can be requested for the
materials.

Objective

Your objective in the game is to persuade other school personnel to side with your view on introducing games into the school
system. Use all the arguments you can muster and all your
powers of persuasion.

Play

1. A copy of the school profile selected for the game is distributed to each player.
2. A profile is distributed to each of the eight (or ten) players.
3. Each player should introduce himself to the group, describing who he is and his basic preference on the issue of games
(one minute each).
4. Next, each player should choose another player at random
to negotiate with. The four (or five) pairs of players will spend
five minutes trying to persuade each other or, if they agree,
developing new arguments to support their position.
5. After five minutes, players rotate to negotiate with the next
player. Every player should discuss the issue with each of the
seven (or nine) other players, for five minutes each.
6. At the end of each discussion, players should record their
estimate of how the other players will vote.
7. At the end of the fifty-minute negotiation session, each
player will have the opportunity to make a final statement in
a last-minute effort to persuade.
8. Players will then record their vote on the Voting Sheet.
Players do not have equal votes. Indicate your vote by placing
the Voting Strength number indicated on your profile under
the appropriate category on the Voting Sheet.

VOTING SHEET

Player	Predicted Vote on Games (including your own)		Actual Vote	
	For	Against	For	Against
Peter Roberts, Teacher				
Phyllis Jones, Teacher				
John Witcomb, Teacher				
Ruth Andrews, Teacher				
Richard Levitt, Principal				
James Reilly, Assistant Superintendent				
Roger Backus, School Committee				
William McAdams, Assistant Principal				
Joseph Adderly, Parent				
Mrs. Lew Wilson, Parent				

Outcome

To determine whether or not your school will adopt games for the coming school year, tally the Voting Strength numbers. Winners are those players whose initial vote corresponds to the policy outcome.

Postgame Discussion

After the game has been played, players should discuss persuasion strategies, reasons for upholding or altering their positions, strengths of the various arguments for and against games, accuracy of predicting other people's views and actions. The game situation should be compared with the players' real-world environment in terms of school characteristics, political structure of the school, receptivity to new ideas, and so forth.

If the game is played more than once, with different profiles, compare the outcomes in terms of the different arguments used based on the differences in the school populations. Were any arguments more persuasive for slow students than for bright? Or the reverse? Did the size of the school have any measurable impact on the policy decision? Did any players change their positions more readily, or less readily, depending on the nature of the school?

Scenarios and Profiles

The basic ten player profiles can be used with any one of the six school profiles as described below.

School Profiles

1. James MacDonald Junior High School

James MacDonald Junior High School is located in the town of Jamesville, a suburb of the southern city of Chelton. Jamesville is a middle-class community of 15,000, composed mainly of white-collar workers and junior executives. The major growth in Jamesville has occurred in the last ten years, and it seems likely that it will continue. Most of the residents own their own homes, but live unpretentiously. There is fairly active parental interest in the school system.

Seven hundred and fifty students attend MacDonald Junior High, which is ten years old. The school is predominantly white, and offers a standard junior high program, including languages. The school clearly could use some improvements and a major enlargement. Last year the increased number of students necessitated a two-shift school day. Many parents objected to the development, but the decision of school officials prevailed. It is widely hoped that the building of a new junior high or an enlargement will relieve the crowding and end the split shift. But at the present time, the school is operating under less than ideal conditions. One favorable aspect of the situation is the fact that the school system is fairly autonomous. There are some state funds available, provided the school can show valid need for them. Determination of how the money is to be spent will then rest with the town's board of education.

The school atmosphere is good, with administration and faculty generally interested in the quality of education being provided. Pride in the school, with that intangible school spirit, has declined somewhat under the strain of the split session. But the decline need not be permanent.

2. Robert E. Lee Elementary School

The Robert E. Lee Elementary School is located in Calumet, a suburb of the southern city of Chelton. Twenty thousand people live in Calumet, an upper-middle-class community of professional people. The town has maintained an air of luxury and exclusiveness despite some population increase over the past decade. The community has many assets, including a good school system. Education receives considerable parental support, even pressure. College consciousness is high, and a major concern among parents of school-age children.

Robert E. Lee is a modern school, six years old, with a gym, good library, and large cafeteria. Classes average fifteen to twenty students each. Emphasis is placed on the individual, and various resources are available to the student having academic or other difficulties. The faculty has not been as adventuresome as it might be, but it has done a commendable job of preparing students for secondary schooling. The community seems generally satisfied with the level of teaching at Robert E. Lee.

3. Benjamin Willis Senior High School

The Benjamin Willis Senior High School is located in the eastern city of Potford, population 1,000,000. The student body is drawn from a fifty-square-block area on the east side, an area composed of middle and lower income groups. The middle-class section, with fairly modern apartment buildings and well-kept streets, merges with a decaying neighborhood of dilapidated dwellings and poorly maintained facilities. The contrast is equally sharp between the standards of living and livelihoods of the residents of the sections.

The school population represents the neighborhood in microcosm. Of the 1800 students, over half are white, the rest black. Willis High offers a general course and a college-preparatory course. The majority of students are in the former track, and about 40 percent in the latter. Many of the college-prep students continue their education beyond high school, and the rest take jobs. Most students in the general course begin working shortly after graduation. Less than 10 percent of the students drop out of school before graduation. The school itself is twenty-nine years old, but is in good condition. Though there is some overcrowding, it is not severe. Most classes number thirty students. A few years ago an addition was made to the building, housing a band room, a modern cafeteria, and a science laboratory. There are some extracurricular activities, including sports teams, school magazine, choir, and band. These activities attract about one-fifth of the students. Yet with each year there is a little more school spirit, and it is hoped that the activities can be increased to attract more students. Parent involvement is low, but has been increasing.

Though the school is dependent on the state for all funds for materials, the administration has been fairly successful in obtaining funds. The state board's control over curriculum has also been circumvented to a small degree. But clearly the school's autonomy is limited by the state's control.

The teaching in the school is mostly traditional, though there has been some experimentation. As in other large schools, importance is placed on discipline and attentiveness. The faculty seems interested and devoted and genuinely concerned with providing a decent education. The administration also appears to take an active interest in the quality of education.

4. Peter Falk Elementary School

The Peter Falk Elementary School is located in the midwestern city of Medderton, population 450,000. Medderton is an industrial city that has experienced a boom in the last twenty years. The population has soared, with many inhabitants coming from the East and the South. The school draws its students from the northern section of the city, currently undergoing extensive urban-renewal projects. Thousands of families have already been moved from slums to city-provided low-income housing.

Five hundred students attend the elementary school, most of them culturally disadvantaged. The school was built four years ago, and is bright and modern. Money for the building came from state and federal funds. The school has also been involved in the Headstart project. In fact, almost half the students have participated in the preschool or summer training programs.

Much remains to be done at Falk Elementary School. Unless the students are reached quickly, they drop behind in learning to read and write, and by the sixth grade are considered failures. There is an air of excitement and interest in the school. Some of the students seem to like school, but there are some serious problems in reaching and teaching all the pupils. The possibility exists of more federal funds for the next few years. Money from the state is also possible, but each request must be reviewed separately. The administration of the school would like more autonomy. The faculty could use further resources to evolve meaningful programs.

5. Thomas P. Franklin Senior High School

The Thomas P. Franklin Senior High School is located in the large eastern city of Potford, population 1,000,000. The student body is drawn from an eighty-square-block area in the upper west side. The lower-class area is characterized by crowded tenements, large public-housing developments, declining small businesses, and few recreational facilities. The crime rate is high and there is little sense of community.

The school has a student body of 2500 students, close to two-thirds of them black and one-third white. Most of the students are considered culturally disadvantaged. The school offers a general program, a college-preparatory program, and a vocational program. About one-quarter of the students are in the college-preparatory track, and few of them continue their academic training beyond high school. One-half of the students are enrolled in the general track, and the remaining students are enrolled in the various vocational-training courses. The school dropout rate is high, with nearly 13 percent leaving school before graduation.

Franklin High is desperately in need of change. Classes are overcrowded, ranging from twenty-eight to thirty-six students. The lack of facilities is shocking in this fifty-year-old school. A new science lab is needed. The gym could use remodeling. The vocational shops lack new equipment. There is little pride in the school, and little school spirit. Parent involvement is low.

One major problem that the school faces is its dependency on the state for all appropriations. State control over the purchase of all materials and over the curriculum severely limit the autonomy of the school's administration. The lack of funds without special approval makes it difficult to procure new books and experimental facilities.

Most of the teaching is traditional, with emphasis on attentiveness, obedience, and respect. The attitude among students, in general, is that school is something everyone has to go through, but not for real enlightenment or enjoyment. Little in the present school policy or programs would indicate that faculty or administration seriously differ with this widely held notion.

6. Darton Senior High School

Darton Senior High School is located in Darton, a suburb of the western city of Lingo. Darton has about 25,000 residents and is a wealthy upper-class community. Most of the residents are professionals or independently wealthy individuals. The residents have extreme pride in their community and its facilities. Darton's school system is well known throughout the

West. As a group, the parents are well informed and actively interested in the schools.

Darton High School has 1200 students. The school offers a college-preparatory program, with honors and advanced placement classes. A language lab, several new science laboratories, and an outstanding high school library are features of the school. The range of extracurricular activities at Darton is impressive. There are literary publications, athletic teams, language clubs, and service organizations. But there are many able students who take little interest in nonacademic activities. Classes average twenty to twenty-five students. The faculty mirrors the community's concern with college admission, and teaching is geared to preparing students for college. In fact, nearly 90 percent of the students go on to college.

A competitiveness exists at the school among students and teachers. A more relaxed atmosphere with some de-emphasis on college would be in the interest of the students — and of real learning. The administration is aware of the school atmosphere.

Darton has been in the fortunate position of having sufficient resources and autonomy to carry out its policies. Community approval is necessary for appropriations, but no direct control is exerted over curriculum.

Personnel Profiles

1. Mr. Peter Roberts, Teacher

You are the head of the math department, a position you have held for several years. You have enjoyed teaching at your school, and have advanced by dint of hard work. Lately you have felt your prestige slipping, and feel you need something to boost your stock in the principal's eyes. Until now you have been a fairly conservative teacher, doing a good though not terribly exciting job. You are no longer convinced that the tried and true methods work best in teaching. In fact, lately you have viewed the standard pattern of homework, recitation, and test as boring, and fear that your boredom is being picked up by your students.

You see no immediate way out of your disenchantment with your methods, though you would welcome suggestions. But even more important in terms of your career, you would like some major success with which to impress the principal. You have heard that the principal is sold on getting games into the school, and this could be the answer. Yet you realize that scheduling problems, the money issue, and possible depart-

ment resistance could prove a hindrance.
Voting strength: 5

2. Mrs. Phyllis Jones, Teacher

You joined the faculty of your school a year ago. You have had seven years experience teaching at two other schools. You left Jones High School because of the rigid control over the faculty. You were led to believe that this school would be different and you have waited patiently. Your primary teaching objective is to reach and move your students. You feel that once they are turned on, teaching them the subject matter, history and government, is much easier.

Your own interest in the subject matter is strong. This past summer you attended a summer workshop on new teaching techniques which gave you a host of ideas. You had the chance to meet teachers from all over the country, see demonstrations of games and simulations and so on and attend a series of lectures on innovations. You saw several games test-played, and were impressed by the level of excitement generated. So far you have tried several simulations in your class. You are convinced that educational games can serve a valid purpose in your teaching, and are anxious to use more of them. You anticipate some problems, however, in getting permission to spend department funds for the purchase of new materials. You hope to persuade other faculty members to give games a try. You favor them as a motivational device which creates an atmosphere conducive to effective learning. You certainly realize that there is a time and place for them.
Voting strength: 3

3. Mr. John Sitcomb, Teacher

You joined the faculty of the school two years ago. Your training was at a liberal arts college, followed by a year of graduate work at a leading teachers college. You are interested in your subject matter, history, and find teaching very stimulating. The graduate courses in methods, the experience you had student-teaching, and your current teaching have convinced you of the value of using new materials where possible. You believe that learning is fostered by an atmosphere of flexibility, innovation, and creativity. Your main goal is to enable your students to learn most effectively. You feel that games and other materials can help you achieve your goal by motivating the students.

Your experience with games, role playing, and simulations revealed that students responded well to them. They were interested, took more initiative, and were more actively involved in the learning process than usual. More important, you have used games as a way of making concrete to students various abstract principles and ideas. And you believe that in a game-playing situation you have the opportunity to assume a different role towards your students, being able to work with them in a mutually interesting activity.

You know that the introduction of such materials requires playing, so that the game has maximum impact and pertinence. You also know that situations occasionally arise in the playing that you cannot plan for. But you feel that the advantages in motivation far outweigh these slight disadvantages.
Voting strength: 3

4. Miss Ruth Andrews, Teacher

You have been teaching science for ten years, all at the same school. You received no graduate training before teaching, but have taken some academic courses since then to keep your certificate in good order. You find teaching interesting and are very devoted to it. Each year that you teach convinces you more that students learn best by abiding by the rules you set down. You think that reading assignments, carefully directed discussion, nightly homework assignments, and evaluation make students do their work and learn. You actively care about your students, and have always given special help to students having difficulty. In short, you believe that the time-honored methods of teaching are the best. And you personally have mastered these techniques. Your good teaching has been recognized by your students and by other faculty members. Last year you won the school's award as best teacher.

Your reading about recent innovations in education, including games, experimental science and history units, and team teaching has aroused your curiosity and skepticism. You wonder if these innovations would fulfill your objectives as well as your own methods do.

You are not interested in trying these methods unless you can be convinced that they are as effective as your own. You would be interested in discussing this with the assistant principal of your school—a man you respect and generally agree with. You think too much freedom, too much noise, and free-for-all classrooms are the mistaken ideals of many young teachers fresh out of college.
Voting strength: 4

5. Mr. Richard Levitt, Principal

You have been principal of the school for eight years, after working your way up through the ranks. You are well satisfied with your school; your facilities are modern, your school well run, and your faculty generally hardworking. Your major concern as principal is that your school continue to provide a good education for its students. You realize that continued good faculty recruitment is a major asset and feel that there is much desirable about the school system to attract able teachers.

As a teacher and administrator, you have sought ways of improving the quality of the education provided. You personally are committed to the ideas of dynamic change and innovation as a means of keeping the school vital. Over the past few years you have participated in several workshops and were impressed by the potentialities of new materials. Now you wish to introduce some innovations, such as experimental science courses, audio-visual facilities, and games to the faculty and encourage their use in the curriculum. You are aware, though, that the possible expense, scheduling conflicts, and space requirements could hamper your efforts. Despite these problems you feel that innovation has a place in your school; you feel it your duty to spur the effort. To succeed, you will have to convince the school committee and the assistant superintendent. It would help if your assistant principal was on your side. He has always felt that he deserved your job.
Voting strength: 8

6. Mr. James Reilly, Assistant Superintendent

As the assistant superintendent of schools, you occupy a position of considerable prestige in the school hierarchy. Your contact with the schools in your district is continuous, but limited to dealing with administrative personnel. It has been years since you taught class. In the years since you assumed this position, your main role has been in directing the smooth running of the schools. You also serve as liaison with other districts' administrators, and you work closely with parent groups.

Your principal concern is that your district continue to provide a good education within the confines of the funds available from the state. You are well aware of the ferment in education, particularly the many new resources available to the teacher. You have no personal commitment to these innovations, either for or against. But realistically you realize that not much money is available from the state for experimentation. If you can be persuaded that games are effective, and that most school personnel want them, you will throw your weight to them.
Voting strength: 10

7. Mr. Roger Backus, School Committee

You are a member of the five-man school committee, a position you were elected to three years ago. The function of the committee is to make school policy for the schools in the district.

The system is currently undergoing change. A new spirit seems to be developing among faculty members, who are becoming interested in new and different materials.

For years the school committee has been relatively inactive. You have been aware of your group's complacency but have done nothing to encourage new policies and programs. You will face reelection next year, and not only do you wish to serve another term on the committee but you would like to become chairman. You think that by supporting an innovative program, you could win the support of parents and teachers.

But you don't want to be accused of simply pushing your own interests. Whatever program is adopted must be educationally sound. You have always relied on William McAdams, a long-time friend, for his opinion on the quality of materials and validity of methods. Without his support you would hesitate to favor any program. You are going to try to win his support to something new. You would also like to be in agreement with the assistant superintendent.

Voting strength: 7

8. Mr. William McAdams, Assistant Principal

As assistant principal of your school, your main concerns are that the school run smoothly, and that the students receive a satisfactory education. Your work most closely relates to school discipline. Your observations of current teaching and your personal experience years ago have convinced you that the most effective teaching is traditional. You believe that students should have assigned tasks, which they must perform. You want students to learn the basics, and do so as straightforwardly as possible. You also know that discipline is best maintained in such an atmosphere, and you feel that proper discipline is of ultimate importance.

You feel that special materials are superfluous, even if the money is available for it. You are well pleased with the traditional approach, and seriously doubt that new materials can improve teaching and learning effectiveness. Besides, you seriously question the appropriateness of games in the classroom.

You are highly respected by your colleagues. Roger Backus of the school committee relies on you. You've always believed that you should have been promoted to principal over Richard Levitt. You hold no personal grudge. You simply believe that you know more about education, are a better administrator and teacher than he. In spite of this, you generally manage to influence things your way.

Voting strength: 6

9. Mr. Joseph Adderly, Parent

The school system your children attend seems interested in providing the best possible education for its students. At meetings and open school night you have met many faculty members and have been impressed by the dynamic, interested quality of the teachers. You take a fairly active role in the school, and are currently vice-president of the PTA.

You consider yourself an informed, interested parent, aware of trends in education. You have read about changes occurring in education, including audio-visual devices, games, team teaching, and other direct involvement techniques. Your recollections of your own dull schooling a generation ago are still vivid, and you strongly feel that maybe things could be better. From your reading, you feel that your children could profit from the introduction of new techniques into classes where appropriate. You would like to see some experimentation and innovation, provided that the goal of good education is not sacrificed. You also hope that these innovations won't necessitate an increase in taxes to finance a larger school budget.
Voting strength: 1

10. Mrs. Lew Willson, Parent

You are the parent of a high school student. The school system your child attends seems interested in providing a decent education. You actually have little contact with the school. You don't really know what your son is learning, but you do care that he pass all his subjects.

You know that the school is a place where kids go because they have to—that's the way it was for you, too. But you've heard some talk about new ways of teaching that will make kids actually want to go to school. You're skeptical about this idea, but are planning to learn more about it by attending the next PTA meeting. You don't think it's your job to tell the school what to teach, but you are concerned about the fact that these new materials are not usually graded. If they're not graded, how will you or your son or his teacher know how well he's doing in school? And how will his future employer be able to evaluate him?
Voting strength: 1

Games Described in Chapter 3

Game	Subject Level	Developer/ Sponsor	Availability
GET SET 8 games	Reading readiness, elementary	Abt Associates	Houghton Mifflin Co. 2 Park St. Boston, Mass 02107
GITHAKA MARKET PLACE FINDING A MATE THE TRACKING GAME SURVIVAL GAME TOOL GAME HUNTING GAME CORN GAME CARGO GAME POLITICS IN BENIN	Social studies, elementary	Abt Associates for EDCOM Systems	Information from: EDCOM Systems Witherspoon St. Princeton, N.J. 08540
MARKET ECONOMY	Economics, elementary	Abt Associates for: Industrial Relations Center Univ. of Chicago	Information from: IRC Univ. of Chicago Chicago, Ill. 60637
KOLKHOZ SIERRA LEONE (Manual version)	Economics, elementary	Abt Associates for: Bd. of Cooperative Educational Services	Information from: BOCES 845 Meadow Road Yorktown Heights, N.Y. 10598
SEAL HUNTING BUSHMAN EXPLORING AND GATHERING CARIBOU	Social studies, elementary	Abt Associates for: Educational Development Center	Information from: EDC 44a Brattle St. Cambridge, Mass. 02138

Game	Subject Level	Developer/ Sponsor	Availability
POLLUTION NEIGHBORHOOD (See Chapter 5 for description)	Social studies, elementary	Abt Associates for: Wellesley School System	Information from: Wellesley Schools Curriculum Center Seawood Road Wellesley, Mass. 02181
COLONY® FRONTIER® RECON- STRUCTION® PROMOTION® INTERVENTION® DEVELOPMENT®	History, junior high	Abt Associates for: Science Research Associates	Available from: Science Research Associates 259 East Erie St. Chicago, Ill. 60611
PURSUIT	Civil rights, history, junior high	Abt Associates for: Reader's Digest	Educational Services Reader's Digest Pleasantville, N.Y. 10570
MATHEMATICS: Cards, Dominoes, Spinners	Math, elementary and junior high	Abt Associates for: D. C. Heath and Co.	D. C. Heath and Co. 125 Spring St. Lexington, Mass. 02173
INTER-NATION SIMULATION	International affairs, secondary	Cherryholmes and Guetzkow Northwestern Univ.	Science Research Associates 259 E. Erie St. Chicago, Ill. 60611
CRISIS	International affairs, secondary	Western Behavioral Sciences Institute	Simile II P.O. Box 1023 La Jolla, Calif. 92037

Game	Subject Level	Developer/ Sponsor	Availability
GRAND STRATEGY	International affairs, history, secondary	Abt Associates	GAMES CENTRAL Abt Associates 55 Wheeler St. Cambridge, Mass. 02138
DANGEROUS PARALLEL	International affairs, secondary	Abt Associates for: Foreign Policy Assoc.	Scott, Foresman and Company 1900 E. Lake Glenview, Ill. 60025
LIFE-CAREER GENERATION GAP ASSOCIATION CONSUMER COMMUNITY DISASTER	Group behavior, sociology, secondary	Dept. of Social Relations Johns Hopkins Univ.	Western Publishing 850 Third Av. New York, N.Y.
RAID	Group behavior, urban crime, secondary	Abt Associates	Games Central Abt Associates 55 Wheeler St. Cambridge, Mass. 02138
PROPAGANDA	Social studies, secondary	Robert Allen, Nova Schools	Maret Company 1111 Maple Av. Turtle Creek, Pa. 15145 or WFF'N PROOF® P.O. Box 71 New Haven, Conn. 06500
PLANS	Social studies, secondary	Western Behavioral Science Institute	Simile II P.O. Box 1023, La Jolla, Calif. 92037

Game	Subject Level	Developer/ Sponsor	Availability
SECTION	Social studies, secondary	Abt Associates for: High School Geography Project	The Macmillan Company School Division 866 Third Av. New York, N.Y. 10022
NAPOLI	Social studies, secondary	Western Behavioral Sciences Institute	Simile II P.O. Box 1023 La Jolla, Calif. 92037
STEAM REVOLUTION SLAVE TRADE ADVENTURING MANCHESTER GALAPAGOS	Social studies, history, secondary	Abt Associates for: Educational Development Center	Information from: Abt Associates 55 Wheeler St. Cambridge, Mass. 02138
EMPIRE	Social studies, history, secondary	Abt Associates for: Educational Development Center	KDI Instructional Systems 1810 MacKenzie Columbus, Ohio 43220
MACHINIST	Social studies, career planning, secondary	Abt Associates for: Graduate school of Education Harvard Univ.	Information from: Information Systems for Vocational Decisions Graduate School of Education Harvard Univ. 220 Alewife Brook Pky. Cambridge, Mass. 02138
SUMERIAN FREE ENTERPRISE	Economics, elementary computer versions	Bd. of Cooperative Educational Services	Information from: BOCES 845 Meadow Rd. Yorktown Heights, N.Y. 10598

Bibliography

Computer Mediated Simulations

Bitzer, Donald L. "PLATO: An Electronic Teaching Device," in *Simulation Models for Education:* Fourth Annual Phi Delta Kappa Symposium of Educational Research, N. A. Fattu and E. Stanley, eds. Bloomington, Ind.: Phi Delta Kappa, 1965, pp. 159–72.

Egbert, Robert L. "The Role of Computer Simulation in Education," *Journal of Educational Measurement,* 2:1–3 (1965).

Ingraham, L. W. "Teachers, Computers and Games: Innovations of the Social Studies," *Social Education,* 31:51–53 (1967).

Leonard, J. M., and Wing, R. L. "Advantages of Using a Computer in Some Kinds of Educational Games," *Institute of Electrical and Electronic Engineers Transactions on Human Factors in Electronics,* 8:75–81 (1967).

"New Equipment and Materials: Computerized Simulation," *Educational Technology,* April 30, 1968, 18–19.

Wing, Richard L., et al. *The Production and Evaluation of Three Computer-Based Economics Games for the Sixth Grade.* Yorktown Heights, N.Y.: The Board of Cooperative Educational Services, June 1967.

Educational Planning and Administration

Abt Associates Inc. *Design for an Elementary and Secondary Education Cost-Effectiveness Model;* vol. 1, Model description. Cambridge, Mass.: Abt, June 1967.

——. *Design for an Elementary and Secondary Education Cost-Effectiveness Model;* vol. 2, The User's Guide. Cambridge, Mass.: Abt, June 1967.

——. *The Use of Planning Simulations and Cost-Effectiveness Modeling in Educational Management Seminars.* Cambridge, Mass.: Abt, April 1968.

Cogswell, John F., et al. *Analysis of Instructional Systems: Final Report,* Santa Monica, Calif.: System Development Corp. and the Office of Education, U.S. Dept. of Health, Education, and Welfare, April 1966.

——. *New Solutions to Implementing Instructional Media Through Analysis and Simulation of School Organization.* Santa Monica, Calif.: System Development Corp., March 1964.

Egbert, Robert L. *Simulation: A Vehicle for Facilitating Innovation and System Design in Education.* Santa Monica, Calif.: System Development Corp. Sept. 1962.

Feldt, Allan G. "Operational Gaming in Planning Education," *Journal of the American Institute of Planners,* 22:17–24 (1966).

Hemphill, J. K.; Griffiths, D. E.; and Frederiksen, N. *Administrative Performance and Personality: A Study of the Principal in a Simulated Elementary School.* New York: Bureau of Publications, Teachers College, Columbia University, 1962.

Kothera, Richard. *A Criterion and Set of Reality-Based Problems for Simulation in Special Education Administration.* Lawrence: University of Kansas, May 1967.

Sage, Daniel D. *The Development of Simulation Materials for Research and Training in Administration of Special Education: Final Report.* Washington, D.C.: Bureau of Education for the Handicapped, U.S. Office of Education, November 1967.

Vandermeer, A. W. "Systems Analysis and Media–A Perspective," *Audio-visual Communication Review,* 12:292–301 (1964).

Elementary School

Allender, Jerome S., et al. *The Teaching of Inquiry Skills to Fifth Grade Children.* Oxford, Ohio: Miami University, February 1968.

Allender, Jerome S. *A Theory for the Teaching of Inquiry.* Oxford, Ohio: Miami University, 1967.

Chicago Public Schools. *Communication Skills Games, Techniques, and Devices for Kindergarten, Grades 1, 2, 3.* Chicago: Chicago Public Schools, 1964.

Leonard, J. M. and Wing, R. L. "Advantages of Using A Computer in Some Kinds of Educational Games," *Institute of Electrical and Electronic Engineers Transactions on Human Factors in Electronics,* 8:75–81 (1967).

Wagner, Guy, and Hosier, Max. *Building Listening Skills with Instructional Games.* Darien, Conn.: Teachers Publication, 1962.

———. *Reading Games: Strengthening Reading Skills with Instructional Games.* Darien, Conn.: Teachers Publication, 1960.

Game Theory

Atkinson, R. C., and Suppes, P. "An Analysis of Two-Person Game Situations in Terms of Statistical Learning Theory," *Journal of Experimental Psychology,* 55 (1958).

Chapman, Laura Hill. *Preliminary Work: An Educational Theory Based on Game Theory.* Columbus: Bureau of Educational Research and Service, Ohio State University.

Kahn, Herman, and Mann, Irwin. *Game Theory.* Santa Monica, Calif: RAND Corp., July 1957.

Stark, G. K. "Games Theory in Education," *School and Society,* 96:43–44 (1968).

General References

Abt Associates Inc. *Game Learning and Disadvantaged Groups.* Cambridge, Mass.: Abt, 1965.

Abt, Clark C. "Education is Child's Play," in *Inventing Education for the Future,* Werner Z. Hirsch, et al. San Francisco: Chandler, 1967, pp. 123–55.

———. "Games for Learning," in *Simulation Games in Learning,* Sarane S. Boocock and E. O. Schild, eds. Beverly Hills, Calif.: Sage Publications, 1968, pp. 65–83.

———. "Games Pupils Play–Why Educational Games Win Converts," *Nation's Schools,* 80:92–93, 118 (1967).

———. *Simulation and the Group.* Paper read at conference sponsored by the Commission of Educational Media of the Association for Supervision and Curriculum Development, NEA, Boston. Cambridge, Mass.: Abt, October 1968.

Allen, Robert W. "The Fourth 'R'" *California Journal of Educational Research,* 16:75–79 (1965).

———. *A Study Conducted at the Burbank Unified School, Burbank, Calif.*: Burbank Unified School District, 1964.

Attig, J. C. "Use of Games as a Teaching Technique," *Social Studies,* 58:25–29 (1967).

Beck, Isabel. *Simulation: Designs for Involvement.* Los Angeles: Southwest Regional Laboratory, May 1968.

Bogdanoff E. et al. *Simulation: An Introduction to a New Technology.* Santa Monica, Calif.: System Development Corp., March 1960.

Boocock, Sarane. "An Experimental Study of the Learning Effects of Two Games with Simulated Environments," *American Behavioral Scientist* 10:8–18 (1966).

———. "Games Change What Goes on in the Classroom," *Nations Schools,* 80:94–95 (1967)

Boocock, Sarane S., and Schild, E. O., eds. *Simulation Games in Learning.* Beverly Hills, Calif.: Sage Publications, 1968.

Boocock, Sarane S.; Schild, E. O.; and Stoll, Clarice. *Simulation and Control Beliefs.* Baltimore: Johns Hopkins, November 1967.

Boocock, Sarane S., et al. *Simulation Games Program: Annual Report.* Baltimore: Johns Hopkins, May 1968.

Carlson, Elliot. "Games in the Classroom," *Saturday Review,* 50:62–5, 82–3 (1967).

Cherryholmes, Cleo H. "Some Current Research on Effectiveness of Educational Simulations: Implications for Alternative Strategies," *American Behavioral Scientist,* 10:4–8 (1966).

Chesler, M., and Fox, R. *Role-Playing Methods in the Classroom.* Chicago: Science Research Associates, 1966.

Christine, Charles. and Christine, Dorothy. "Simulation, A Teaching Tool," *The Elementary School Journal,* 67:396–98 (1967).

Coleman, James S. "Academic Games and Learning," in *Proceedings of the 1967 Invitational Conference on Testing Problems.* Princeton: Educational Testing Service, 1968, pp. 67–75.

———. *The Adolescent Society.* Glencoe, Ill.: Free Press, 1961.

———. "Games: New Tools for Learning," *Scholastic Teacher,* 51:9 (November 1967).

———. "In Defense of Games." *American Behavioral Scientist,* 10:3–4 (1966).

———. "Learning Potential in Games," *Michigan Educational Journal,* 45:52 (1968).

———. "Learning Through Games," *National Education Association Journal,* 56:69–70 (1967).

Colorado, University of. *Role Playing Simulation in Instruction*. Boulder, Colo.: Tape Duplicating Service, National Tape Repository, 1966.

Crawford, Meredith P. "Simulation in Training and Education." Paper presented at NATO Symposium on the Simulation of Human Behavior, Paris, July 1967. Alexandria, Va.: Human Resources Research Office, George Washington University, September 1967.

Davis, O. L., Jr. "Simulation: Looking Toward the Future." Paper presented at conference sponsored by the Commission on Educational Media of the Association for Supervision and Curriculum Development, NEA, Boston. Austin: University of Texas, October 1968.

Egerton, John. "Academic Games: Play as You Learn," *Southern Education Report*, March-April 1966.

Farran, Dale C. "Games Work with Underachievers," *Scholastic Teacher*, 5:10–11 (November 1967).

Fattu, Nicholas A. "An Introduction to Simulation," in *Simulation Models for Education: Fourth Annual Phi Delta Kappa Symposium on Educational Research*, N. A. Fattu and E. Stanley, eds. Bloomington, Ind.: Phi Delta Kappa, 1965, 1–24.

Fattu, Nicholas A., and Stanley, E., eds. *Simulation Models for Education: Fourth Annual Phi Delta Kappa Symposium on Educational Research*. Bloomington, Ind.: Phi Delta Kappa, 1965.

Fleck, Henrietta. "Educational Games," *Forecast for Home Economics* 13:57, 103–4 (1967).

"Games for the Classroom," *Scholastic Teacher*, Nov. 9, 1967, 12–13.

Geriach, V. S. "Academic Games and Simulation in Instruction," *Audiovisual Instruction*, 12:609–10 (1967).

Guss, Carolyn. "Role-playing Simulation in Instruction," *Audiovisual Instruction*, 11:443–44 (1966).

Kasperson, Roger E. "Games as Educational Media," *Journal of Geography*, 62:409–22 (1968).

Klietsch, Ronald G., and Dodge, Dorothy. *An Introduction to Learning Games and Instructional Simulations: Curriculum Guidelines*. Newport, Minn.: Instructors Simulations, 1968.

McLuhan, Marshall. "Games, The Extensions of Man," in *Understanding Media: The Extensions of Man*. New York: McGraw-Hill, 1964.

Mulially, Genevieve. "Games in the Classroom," *Montana Education*, February 1968, 40–42.

"National Center Encourages Use of Academic Gaming," *Scholastic Teacher*, Nov. 9, 1967.

National Gaming Council. *The Gaming Newsletter*. Four issues. Washington, D.C.: Environmetrics, 1969-70.

Plumpton, Russell A. *Methods of Determining Pupil Readiness for Specific Units of Instruction Through Simulated Environment Media: Final Report*. Bedford Hills, N.Y.: Board of Cooperative Educational Services, June 1964.

Robinson, James A. "Simulation and Games," in *The New Media and Education: Their Impact on Society*, P. H. Rossi and B. J. Biddle, eds. Garden City, N.Y.: Doubleday, 1967, pp. 93–135.

Ryan, T. Antoinette. "Use of Simulation to Increase Transfer," *School Review*, 76:246–52 (June 1968).

Serious Games. New York: Viking Press, 1970.

Smith, J. P. "Academic Games in the Classroom, *School and Society*, 96:184–85 (1968).

Twelker, Paul A. "Designing Simulation Systems." Paper presented at the American Educational Research Association Convention, Los Angeles, February 1969. Monmouth: Teaching Research, Oregon State System of Higher Education, 1969.

———. "Simulation: What is It? Why is It?" Paper presented at the conference, Simulation: Stimulation for Learning, sponsored by the Commission of Educational Media for the Association for Supervision and Curriculum Development, NEA, at San Diego, California, April 1968. Monmouth: Teaching Research, Oregon State System of Higher Education, April 1968.

Twelker, Paul A., ed. *Instructional Simulation Systems: An Annotated Bibliography*. Corvallis: Continuing Education Publications, 1969.

Wagner, Guy. "What Schools Are Doing: Using Challenging Learning Activities," *Education*, 86:379–81 (1966).

Wing, Richard L. "Simulation as a Method of Instruction in Science Education," *Science Teacher*, 35:41–42 (May 1968).

Math and Science

Dumas, Enoch. *Arithmetic Games*. San Francisco: Fearon, 1960.

Vivian, Charles. *Science Games for Children*. New York: Sterling, 1963.

Secondary Level Simulations

Boocock, Sarane S. "Changing the Structure of Secondary Education with Simulated Environments," *Educational Technology*, 8:3–6 (1968).

——. *Effects of Election Campaign Game in Four High School Classes: Report No. 7*. Baltimore: Research Program in the Effects of Games with Simulated Environments in Secondary Education, Johns Hopkins, 1963.

Boocock, Sarane S., and Coleman, James S. "Games with Simulated Environments in Learning," *Social Education*, 39:215–63 (1966).

Cherryholmes, Cleo H. *Developments in Simulation of International Relations for High School Teaching*. Unpublished master's thesis. Emporia: Kansas State Teachers College, 1963.

Coleman, James S., et al. *Research Program in the Effects of Games with Simulated Environments in Secondary Education*. Baltimore: Department of Social Relations, Johns Hopkins, October 1964.

Garvey, Dale M., and Seiler, William H. *A Study of Effectiveness of Different Methods of Teaching International Relations to High School Students: Final Report*. Emporia: Kansas State Teachers College, February 1966.

Gelatt, H. B. and Varenhorst, Barbara. "A Decision-Making Approach to Guidance," *National Association of Secondary School Principals Bulletin*, 52:88–98 (1968).

Grambs, J. D.; Iverson, W. J., and Patterson, F. K. "Discussion and Role-Playing," in *Modern Methods in Secondary Education*,

rev. ed. New York: Dryden Press, 1958, pp. 252–315.

Gumbrell, Arthur J. "Simulation as a Teaching Tool," *California Teachers Association Journal*, 63:11–13 (1967).

Sybouts, W. "Simulation: An Added Dimension to Student Council Leadership Training," *School Activities* 38:14 (1967).

Western Behavioral Sciences Institute. *A Study of Educational Uses of Simulation*. La Jolla, Calif: WBSI, February 1966.

Yount, Dave, and DeKock, Paul. "Simulations and the Social Studies: The Use of Game Theory in Teaching U.S. History," in *Innovations in the Social Studies: Teachers Speak for Themselves*, Dale L. Brubaker. New York: Crowell, 1968.

Social Sciences

Baker, Eugene H. *A Comparative Study Using Textbook and Simulation Approaches in Teaching Junior High American History*. A doctoral dissertation. Evanston, Ill.: Northwestern University.

Boocock, Sarane S. "Innovation in the Social Studies: Prospects and Problems." Paper presented at the Fall Conference of the Pennsylvania Council for the Social Studies, September 1967.

Cohen, Bernard C. "Political Gaming in the Classroom," *Journal of Politics*, 24:367–81 (1962).

Garvey, Sancha K. "An Annotated Bibliography of Simulation, Role-Playing, and Sociodrama in the Social Studies," *Emporia State Research Studies*, 16:22–34 (1967).

Joint Council on Economic Education. *Bibliography of Games-Simulations for Teaching Economics and Related Subjects*. New York: JCEE, January 1968.

Nesbit, William A. "Simulation Games for the Social Studies Classroom," *New Dimensions*, 1 (1968).

Western Behavioral Sciences Institute. *A Study of Educational Uses of Simulation*. La Jolla, Calif: WBSI, February 1966.

Yount, Dave, and DeKock, Paul. "Simulations and the Social Studies: The Use of Game Theory in Teaching U.S. History," in *Innovations in the Social Studies: Teachers Speak for Themselves*, Dale L. Brubaker. New York: Crowell, 1968.

Sources of Games

Abt Associates Inc. *Game List*. Cambridge: Abt

Boocock, Sarane S. "Simulation Games Today," *Educational Technology*, 8:7–10 (1968).

"Games for the Classroom," *Scholastic Teacher*, November 9, 1967, 12–13.

Johns Hopkins University. *Simulation Games*. Baltimore: Johns Hopkins.

Joint Council on Economic Education. *Bibliography of Games-Simulations for Teaching Economics and Related Subjects*. New York: JCEE, January 1968.

University Council for Educational Administration. *Instructional Materials*. Columbus, Ohio: UCEA, August 1, 1967.

Zieler, Richard. *Games for School Use*. Yorktown Heights, N. Y.: Center for Educational Services and Research, Board of Cooperative Educational Services, March 1968.

Vocational Education

Abt Associates Inc. *System Analysis and Educational Simulation of 20 Years of the Machinist's Vocation*. Cambridge: Abt, July 1967.

Antrim, William H. "Realistic Learning in a Simulated Environment," *American Vocational Journal* 42:29–31 (1967).

Babb, Emerson M., and Eisgruber, Ludwig M. *Management Games for Teaching and Research*. Chicago: Educational Methods, 1966.

Oen, Urban T. *Simulation: A New Dimension in Vocational Education*. East Lansing: Research and Development Program in Vocational-Technical Education, Department of Secondary Education and Curriculum, Michigan State University, May 1968.

Game Development Centers

Games Central
Abt Associates Inc.
55 Wheeler Street
Cambridge, Mass.

Department of Social Relations
Johns Hopkins University
Baltimore, Maryland

Academic Games Project
Nova Schools
Fort Lauderdale, Florida

Teaching Research
Oregon State System of Higher Education
Monmouth, Oregon

Western Behavioral Sciences Institute
1211 Torrey Pine Road
La Jolla, California

The text
of *Games for Growth*
was composed on Linofilm in
9-point Optima by Applied Typographic
Systems of Palo Alto. This typeface, which
is between a classic roman and a sans serif, was
introduced in 1958 by the German type designer,
Hermann Zapf, who has produced over
fifty typefaces since 1939, including
Palatino, Melior, and Janson.
Printing and binding of
this book were done by
Peninsula Lithographic
Co., Menlo Park.